Ines Scheurmann

Water Plants
in the Aquarium

Choosing, Planting, Care, Propagation, and Technology
With a Special Chapter on Decorating
Your Home or Apartment with Plant Aquariums
and Paludariums

Translated from the German by
Elizabeth D. Crawford

American Consulting Editor
Thomas D. Johnson, PhD

With Color Photographs by well-known Plant
Photographers, and Drawings by György Jankovics

BARRON'S

New York • London • Toronto • Sydney

Note and Warning

This book describes electrical equipment used in the care of plants and aquariums. Follow the advice on page 15 exactly to avoid accidents that can have very grave consequences. Make absolutely sure that neither children nor grown-ups eat any of the aquarium plants, or serious injuries to health could result. If you are preparing an aquarium for the first time, remember that approximately 1 quart (1 L) of water weighs 2.2 pounds (1 kg) and that a filled tank of the largest size given in this book can therefore weight more than 750 pounds (350 kg). Check the weight-bearing capacity of the floor of the room where the aquarium will be, and make sure you have an absolutely firm and even supporting surface, because unevenness can result in broken glass and considerable water damage.

English translation © Copyright 1987
by Barron's Educational Series, Inc.

© Copyright 1987 by Gräfe and Unzer
GmbH, Munich, West Germany
The title of the German book is *Wasserpflanzen im Aquarium*

All rights reserved.
No part of this book may be reproduced in any form,
by photostat, microfilm, xerography, or any other means,
or incorporated into any information retrieval system, electronic
or mechanical, without the written permission of
the copyright owner.

All inquiries should be addressed to:
Barron's Educational Series, Inc.
250 Wireless Boulevard
Hauppauge, NY 11788

Library of Congress Catalog Card No. 87-19605

International Standard Book No. 0-8120-3926-2

Library of Congress Cataloging-in-Publication Data

Scheurmann, Ines, 1950-
    Water plants in the aquarium.

    Translation of: Wasserpflanzen im Aquarium.
    Subtitle: Choosing, planting, care, propagation, and
technology, with a special chapter on decorating your home or
apartment with plant aquariums and paludariums.
    Includes index.
    1. Aquarium plants.   I. Title.   II. Title: Waterplants in the
aquarium.
SF457.7.S3413   1988   635.9'674   87-19605
ISBN 0-8120-3926-2

PRINTED IN THE UNITED STATES OF AMERICA
789   490   987654321

Born in 1950, **Ines Scheurmann** is a graduate biologist (speciality: fish behavior), and has many years of practical experience in the keeping and propagation of aquarium plants and fish. She is the author of *The New Aquarium Handbook*.

Photo credits

Brünner: pages 10 (bottom center; bottom right), 19 (top left; bottom left); 20 (top); Kahl: pages 9, 29 (top right; bottom), 39 (back cover, top right); Möhlmann: pages 10 (top right), 20 (bottom); Paffrath: inside front cover, pages 10 (top left; top center; center left; center center; center right; bottom left), 19 (top center; top right; center left; center center; center right; bottom center; bottom right), 29 (top left); 30 (top left; top center; top right; center left; center center; center right; bottom left; bottom center), inside back cover and back cover (top left; bottom left; bottom right); Reinhard: front cover, pages 30 (bottom right); 40 (top; bottom left; bottom right).

The color photos on the covers show

Front cover: plant aquarium with neon tetras (*Paracheirodon innesi*). In the left foreground, fanwort (*Cabomba caroliniana*); right foreground, *Echinodorus horemanni;* behind, water sprite (*Ceratopteris thalictroides*).

Inside front cover: *Barclaya longifolia*.

Inside back cover: example of a plant aquarium. Right foreground: lizard's-tail (*Saururus cernuus*) ascending toward the back; center: right, *Rotala macrandra*; left, water hyssop (*Bacopa caroliniana*), in front, *Micranthemum umbrosum*.

(*Ludwigia repens*); top right, sword plant (*Echinodorus cordifolius*); bottom left, *Salvinia auriculata*; bottom right, *Rotala macrandra*.

Contents

Preface

An aquarium can become the decorative focal point of a room, but only if the plants are attractive and thriving. It is easier than you may think to create an underwater world that is an object of fascination and wonder to all who see it. To be successful, however, the aquarist must know the precise needs of the water plants and understand the plants' vital function as producers of oxygen and purifiers of water in the aquarium.

In this book, the author, an experienced aquarist, gives advice and direction for the proper choice of plants and optimum care of them so that all aquarium inhabitants — the plants and the fish — can thrive at the same time. She gives tried and true tips for the proper fertilization and successful propagation of water plants. One detailed chapter describes how to set up the aquarium intelligently to best meet the basic survival needs of the inhabitants — that is, warmth, clean water, and light. All suggestions are so easy to understand that even a beginner can carry them out.

Here the aquarist is offered choices of four popular forms and advised as to the planning and care required for each:
- the fish aquarium with attractive water plants,
- the plant aquarium "trimmed" with small fish,
- the open aquarium with small fish and with plants that rise above the water surface and bloom there,
- the paludarium, in which water, swamp, and land plants unite to form an impressive and to some extent even a blooming plant community.

A strong point of this book is the large special chapter (Aquarium Plants, see page 56), in which 60 of the most beautiful water and swamp plants are described and pictured. The precise details of appearance, light needs, water condition, and care requirements, as well as advice for placement of the plants in the aquarium, enable even beginners to put together an attractive, well-functioning plant collection. The detailed advice on care, the informative plant drawings, and the many color photographs make it easy to enlarge already-existing plant stands attractively or to plant a new aquarium decoratively.

There are seldom illnesses in aquarium plants, but mistakes in the choice of plants, fertilization, and care can produce damage. The chapter Plant Damage and Ailments contains much advice on how to recognize the causes of disturbances in the aquarium and how to remedy them.

In a well-maintained aquarium, in which the plants are growing well, producing oxygen, and keeping the water clean, the fish will also prosper, show their natural behavior, and perhaps even reproduce.

Author and publisher thank all who have been involved in furnishing this book with extraordinary color photographs and the informative drawings: botanical artists György Jankovics and the plant photographers listed on page 2, especially Kurt Paffrath, Burkard Kahl, and Hans Reinhard. Special thanks for the expert advice and review of the manuscript are owed to Messrs Konrad Helbig, Gera/Thüringen, and Peter Stadelmann, Nuremberg.

Water Plants and Their Needs

Why Plants Are Important in the Aquarium

A beautifully planted aquarium is a fascinating eye-catcher. However, the plants in the aquarium are not merely decorative; they play a crucial role in the maintenance of life: if they are healthy, they produce oxygen, take up the carbon dioxide expelled by the fish, and help to break down waste materials. In doing so, the plants make a vital contribution to the creation of a stable aquarium milieu and thus one that is highly beneficial to fish.

With the help of their chlorophyll, the material that makes leaves green, the plants can use the sunlight as an energy source. With the aid of chlorophyll, they synthesize carbohydrates from water and carbon dioxide and from the carbohydrates they synthesize starch and cellulose. Through this process, which is called photosynthesis, oxygen is released — a by-product of this process.

Because the oxygen that we breathe is produced by chlorophyll-containing plants, namely the algae, mosses, ferns, and blooming plants, neither we nor other animals can live without plants. Only when the first single-celled algae developed chlorophyll after some two and a half to three billion years could the development of animal life forms also begin. Before that there were only microorganisms and bacteria, which managed with the meager oxygen of the original atmosphere or could live without it entirely. As time passed, plants (and later animals, too) went through many adaptations of bodies and organs to allow them to live outside the water, and they settled on land.

Plants not only photosynthesize and thereby give off oxygen, but they also breathe. Just like animals they respire — breathing oxygen in and carbon dioxide out.

Photosynthesis only takes place when there is sufficient light. Thus plants can only photosynthesize and produce oxygen if they have enough light. Respiration proceeds at about the same rate day and night. At night or in poor lighting, the plants in a crowded aquarium compete with the fish for oxygen.

Plants can do more than just produce oxygen:

- In the aquarium they clean the water of waste materials that are present from fish feces and urine or from fish food. The nitrogenous substances that are thus produced are broken down by the plants and used as fertilizer.
- Many plants contain bactericidal materials, with which they can make water polluted with bacteria habitable for fish again.
- Healthy plants give off a little oxygen in the area around their roots, so that the soil does not become sour.
- Bacteria and small algae settle on the plants, which also can purify the water.

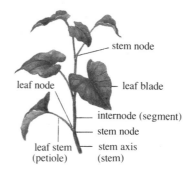

The important parts of a stem plant (plants with extended stem axes).

The Structure of Plants

The largest and best-developed group of aquarium plants is the one containing the flowering plants. They have roots, stems,

5

Water Plants and Their Needs

leaves, and flowers, they reproduce by seeds, and they possess complicated supply and support systems composed of highly differentiated types of cells. Mosses, ferns, and, especially, algae are substantially simpler in structure.

Flowering plants

The above-ground stem of the flowering plants consists of the stem axis, the leaves, and the flowers. The *stem axis* is what botanists call the main stem of each plant, whether they are talking about the tender stem of a *Limnophila* species or about the trunk of a giant sequoia (*Metasequoia gigantea*). The tip of the stem is the growth zone of the plant and is called the vegetative point or vegetative cone. Stems may be elongated, but they may also be foreshortened.

alternate   decussate   whorled   ground-level
                                                        rosette

Leaf arrangement in stem plants: alternate, decussate, and whorled. With rosettes (plants with foreshortened stem axes) the leaves form a rosette at ground level (far right).

Stem plants have an elongated stem on which the leaves occur at intervals large enough that the stem can be seen in between.

Rosette plants have a foreshortened stem. The stem is not seen; the leaves are so close together that they appear to be a rosette of leaves arising from the ground.

The leaves arise from the stem. They consist of the blade (the part we describe as "leaf") and the leaf stem (petiole). In plants with elongated stems, the point at which the leaves arise is often thickened. These are called nodes (from Latin *nodi*). The leafless part of the stem between nodes is called the internode, or segment. From the leaf axes (see drawing on page 5) are developed the side branches of the stem.

The leaves can be arranged on the stem in various ways: whorled, opposite, decussate, and alternate.

On the upper side of the leaf blade (and also on green leaf stems and green stems) are located the chlorophyll-containing cells in which photosynthesis is carried out. On the underside of the leaf are the stomata, which the plant can cause to open or close. Gas exchange with the environment is accomplished through these openings: oxygen (O_2) and carbon dioxide (CO_2) are taken up and given off and water vapor is expired.

The roots anchor the plant in the soil and take up nutrients from the soil.

Storage organs: The sugars produced by photosynthesis are usually converted to starch in the leaves. Part of this is stored in the leaves, part in the stem or in special storage organs, and part in the roots. Storage organs in aquatic plants are mostly thickened portions of the underground stem axis, called rhizomes (for example in *Echinodorus* and *Cryptocoryne*), or tubers arising from the stem axis (as in the genus *Aponogeton*) or bulbs (as in the genus *Crinum*).

Adaptation to aquatic life

Aquatic plants possess a very highly developed air-intake system, which extends from the leaves to the outermost tip of the roots. In this way they achieve buoyancy in the water. Since the water supports the plants, their stems and leaves have far less structural tissue than the land plants. If you take an aquarium plant out of the water, it more or less collapses.

The photosynthetic tissue of aquatic plants resembles that of land plants. But aquatic plants do not have the protective sheath over the epidermis, called the cuticle, that keeps the land plants from drying out. Their leaves are so thin and tender that the gases and nutrients can be removed from the water directly across the leaf (and stem) surface.

Adaptation to the natural habitat

Not all aquatic plants live underwater all year long (submerged); many grow in swampy areas or in streams with seasonally lower water levels. For several months every year they stand out of the water (emergent) or at least project above the water surface. During this period they put forth hard, firm above-water leaves (which in structure are similar to those of land plants), and they take in water and nourishment by means of their roots alone. Many of these swamp plants do this in the aquarium, too, even if they are kept submerged there all year around. Therefore they are best placed in ground that has been fertilized beforehand (see page 33).

Swamp plants can be recognized because their submerged leaves appear relatively coarse and are not pinnated.

Typical examples of this are the *Echinodorus* species (swordplants), *Cryptocoryne*, and most of the *Hygrophila* species.

Plants submerged all year are *Egeria* and *Elodea* species and species of *Myrophyllum* (water milfoils) and *Ceratophyllum* (hornwort).

The Requirements of Aquarium Plants

So that the plants in the aquarium remain biologically efficient, produce oxygen, take

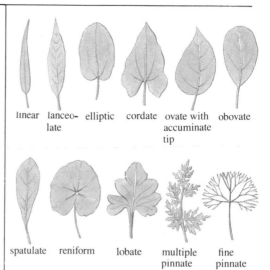

linear lanceolate elliptic cordate ovate with accuminate tip obovate

spatulate reniform lobate multiple pinnate fine pinnate

Various leaf forms—important for the recognition of aquarium plants.

up waste products, and develop their other water-purifying characteristics, they must be properly provided with whatever they need to sustain life. Besides the requirements for light and heat, which will be supplied by means of aquarium technology (see page 15), their life element, the water, must be adjusted to their needs.

Oxygen (O_2)

Animals and plants breathe oxygen (O_2) in and carbon dioxide (CO_2) out. Oxygen is one of the necessities of life for all organisms. The oxygen dissolved in water comes only in part from the air; partly it is produced by the plants during photosynthesis and released into the water. The cooler the water is, the more oxygen it holds. Oxygen in the air dissolves better in water the more vigorously the water surface moves. Rushing brooks are therefore richer in oxygen than standing water.

Water Plants and Their Needs

In the aquarium the excretions of the fish and the remains of the fish food add nitrogen and phosphorous compounds to the water (see page 13). These and many other waste products must be broken down and converted to harmless compounds by the bacteria that inhabit the floor and the filter. To do so the bacteria need abundant oxygen. When there is too little oxygen, the filter is either not working or working too slowly! Oxygen deficiency injures both the fish and the plants (see Nutritional Disturbances, page 52).

Care: The aquarist must try to achieve a concentration of O_2 in the aquarium as close to saturation as possible. This is only possible in a well-planted tank that does not hold too many fish and in which the plants are provided with optimal light, heat, and nourishment. In such tanks the O_2 content can reach more than 100 percent saturation (the theoretical maximum amount of oxygen in the water at a given temperature) during the course of the day, even if in the morning it is only about 40 to 50 percent. At night all the organisms in the aquarium — fish, plants, bacteria — consume the oxygen in the water.

Testing O_2 content: Oxygen test kits, with which you can measure the O_2 content of the aquarium water yourself, can be obtained from scientific supply houses, although they are expensive. In general, it is best to rely upon aeration and healthy plants to maintain adequate oxygen concentrations.

Avoiding maintenance mistakes: The following disturbances to the equilibrium of the aquarium can result in failure to achieve an adequate concentration of oxygen in the water:
- Too few plants or else plants that because of some deficiency do not carry out photosynthesis.
- Too many fish and therefore dirty water.
- Dirty water because of leftover food, dying plants, or other decomposing organic material.
- Floor thickened because of overly-fine sand or silt or by mulm.
- Filter neglected and dirty.

Hint: To guarantee constant provision of nourishment for the plants, slow-release fertilizers on the aquarium floor, liquid fertilizers after each water change (see Fertilization, page 33), and possibly daily addition of trace elements (see page 14) are helpful.

Carbon dioxide (CO_2)

Carbon dioxide (CO_2) is a vital plant nutrient. When CO_2 is deficient, the plants cannot engage in photosynthesis and therefore cannot make oxygen either. CO_2 deficiency thus has the same results in the aquarium as oxygen deficiency, with all the negative consequences for fish and filtering bacteria; almost every plant will grow poorly, even if well fertilized and well lighted.

Care: Fertilizing the plants with carbon dioxide is recommended if you want to promote vigorous growth. In the last few years there have been different methods developed for providing carbon dioxide in aquariums. It is even possible, in some areas, to obtain devices that continually release small amounts of CO_2 into the aquarium from a pressurized bottle (CO_2 diffuser). Constant output is maintained by an electronic measuring and control device. At night the plants only breathe and do not carry on photosynthesis, so they do not need additional CO_2.

Sword plant (*Echinodorus cordifolius*) in an aquarium ▷ with neon tetras (*Paracheirodon innesi*).

Water Plants and Their Needs

The CO_2 diffuser should be connected to the switch that controls the lamp. It turns off the CO_2 diffuser as soon as the light goes out. But even with a simpler apparatus — such as a diffusion bell with a spray bottle — you can stimulate your plants to active growth. Addition of a small amount of seltzer (*not* club soda) occasionally is an acceptable substitute for an automated system.

Monitoring CO_2 content: Besides the drop indicators, a few of the larger pet stores have small testing devices, the so-called CO_2 constancy tests, with which the CO_2 concentrations and the function of any fertilizing equipment can be monitored. These devices are filled with liquid indicators that react to pH changes in the water (see page 12), which can result from too much or too little carbon dioxide. You can also tell anytime by a glance at the color scale whether the tank is optimally provided with CO_2.

Avoiding maintenance mistakes: The very high concentrations of CO_2 required for vigorous growth of aquarium plants can rarely be maintained if the water is rapidly churned. The moving water is advantageous to the fish, on the other hand, for they must somehow get rid of the CO_2 that they expire so that they can breathe in again. In water that is too full of CO_2 they will suffocate. You must bear these different requirements of plants

◁ Attractive water plants. Top left, *Cryptocoryne corda ta*; top center, *Rotala rotundifolia*; top right *Vallisneria asiatica var. biwaensis*.
Center left, water hyssop (*Bacopa caroliniana*); center center, *Aponogeton crispus*; center right, cardinal flower (*Lobelia cardinalis*).
Bottom left, *Cryptocoryne affinis*; bottom center, *Ammania senegalensis*; bottom right, *Ludwigia palustris*.

and animals in mind when you arrange the planting and the inhabitants of your aquarium and choose the filter equipment.

Water hardness

Today even most novice aquarists know that water can be "hard" or "soft." Hardening agents are the salts of calcium and magnesium, primarily. Calcium and magnesium are earth alkaline metals. Water that contains many of these mineral salts is called hard; water that contains little of them is called soft. Aquarists state the water hardness (total hardness) in hardness grades (1° dH corresponds to 10 mg oxide of calcium or magnesium in 1 liter of water). Modern water chemistry utilizes the concept "the sum of earth alkalis" and measures in mols per cubic meter. The following broad categories have come into use:

    0 to 4° dH = very soft water
    5 to 8° dH = soft water
    9 to 12° dH = medium hard water
    13 to 20° dH = hard water

Care: Water with a hardness value of 8 to 16° dH has proven best for the care of most plants and fish. (Our water supply as a rule has 8 to 17° dH.) Only a few tropical plants need softer water, for example *Aponogeton rigidifolius*. For these — and for raising many tropical fish — the water must be softened either with chemicals or, more effectively, with an ion-exchanger. You can learn the hardness grade of your water supply from your waterworks. In case you need to measure it yourself, you can get indicator liquids and measuring equipment in a pet store.

Softening and hardening: If you want to keep fish and plants other than those that are acclimated to the general level of hardness of your water supply, you must harden or soften the water. You can best find out about the exact methods of softening and hardening, such as by use of an ion-exchanger, from a dealer or in books about water chemistry.

Carbonate hardness (Alkalinity)

Not only is the sum of the earth alkalis (total hardness) important for plants; the compounds that calcium and magnesium enter into with carbonic acid are also important. These play a vital role in the nutrient economy of the plant. Carbonic acid is formed when CO_2 dissolves in water. Most of this dissolved gas remains as free CO_2 in solution; only a tiny portion (0.7 percent) combines with water to become carbonic acid. The calcium and magnesium salts of the carbonic acid produce the carbonate hardness. The hardness produced by sulfates and other compounds of magnesium and calcium, is the noncarbonate hardness. The total hardness of aquarium water (the sum of the earth alkalis) is therefore the sum of carbonate hardness and noncarbonate hardness.

Care: Carbonate hardness is very important for plant maintenance (see above), so it is measured separately; measuring reagents with precise instructions for their use are available at the pet store. High carbonate hardness can be reduced by means of an ion-exchanger, peat filter, or CO_2 fertilizer. For a serious deficiency of carbonate hardness (Biogenic decalcification, see below) install a CO_2-fertilizing apparatus.

The pH value

The pH value indicates the acidity of the water. In all natural water there are certain amounts of acidic- and alkaline-reacting substances dissolved. If water contains more acids than alkalis, it is acid, if it contains more alkalis than acids, it is alkaline. If the acids and alkalis are in balance, the water is chemically neutral.

The pH scale ranges from 1 to 14. Neutral water has a pH value of 7. Water with a pH value of less than 7 is acid, water with a pH value of more than 7 is alkaline. The more acid or alkaline it becomes, the further the pH departs from the value of 7 respectively. Most tropical waters are slightly acid, and tropical plants and fish therefore thrive well at pH values of about 5.8 to 7.0.

Care: In many places the water supply has a pH of 6.5 to 7.2. Most aquarium plants can tolerate these values without difficulty. Measure the pH regularly (about every 14 days) with a drop indicator or a pH measuring kit (pet store). For wide fluctuations of pH value (see Biogenic decalcification below) institute CO_2 fertilization or partial water change. For acidifying the water you can use peat preparations if the fish living in the aquarium come from dark water or if you are not growing plants that need a great deal of light.

Carbonate hardness, pH, and plants

Carbonate hardness often undergoes wide fluctuations in the aquarium because of the photosynthetic activities of the plants. This influences the pH value. To understand this process you need to know that the hardening agents calcium and magnesium form two different componds with carbonic acid: bicarbonates and carbonates. Bicarbonates are instable compounds; carbonates are almost insoluble in water. The harder natural water is, therefore, the more CO_2 is bound in bicarbonates and carbonates and the more alkaline it is. Soft water in nature is slightly acidic because it contains only few hardeners that can bind the CO_2.

Biogenic decalcification: Plants that come from regions with more or less soft, slightly acidic water in nature find much free CO_2 in the water and use only this for photosynthesis. Plants from regions with harder water, such as most of the European and North American species, but also many tropical plants, have the capacity to split biocarbonates and to extract the CO_2 from them for their nourishment. When the CO_2 is removed from the bicarbonates, carbonates precipitate on the plant leaves as a rough coating (boiler scale). The pH increases as a result of this biogenic decalcification and the fish get lung alkalosis. Some plants, particularly *Egeria,* can also extract the CO_2 from carbonates. This allows the pH to rise even higher, to life-threatening values for the fish. By night, when no photosynthesis is taking place, the process reverses again, the carbonates become bicarbonates, and the pH values sink into the normal range. This process is particularly dangerous in aquariums that are abundantly planted with *Egeria, Vallisneria,* and *Sagittaria,* since these plants decalcify the water very quickly.

Care: Wide fluctuations of water hardness and pH during the course of a day are not good for the plants, quite apart from the danger to the fish. A well-balanced mixture of plants and regular iron supplements will prevent severe disturbances. In addition you might have to fertilize with CO_2 so that the plants can get enough nourishment from soft water and need not extract the bicarbonates and carbonates from hard water.

Note: The amount of carbonate hardness is much more important for the growth of plants than the amount of noncarbonate hardness; therefore, only the degree of carbonate hardness is given in the plant descriptions.

Nitrogen compounds

Nitrogen is an extremely important plant nutrient. Aquatic plants do not take it in as the gaseous element nitrogen, nor do they readily use nitrates as land plants do, but instead use ammonium. Ammonium only exists in acidic water; it is formed from ammonia, which is present in the water because of elimination from the fish, remains of food, and other organic matter. In the normally lightly acid milieu of our aquarium the ammonium scarcely harms the fish, but in alkaline water it quickly turns into the poisonous ammonia again.

Ammonium or ammonia is converted by the filter bacteria (see page 8) through toxic nitrite to relatively harmless nitrate in a process that uses oxygen. If the plants are not healthy — for instance in an overcrowded aquarium with a neglected filter — they cannot carry on photosynthesis and cannot produce oxygen. The breakdown of nitrogen compounds then takes too long or doesn't occur at all. The result: The fish can die of ammonia or nitrite poisoning.

Care: Maintain the filter carefully and change a portion of the water regularly. In addition, fertilize afterwards regularly because in oxygen-rich water the bacteria will quickly take up the ammonium and convert it to nitrates. Normally the aquatic plant fertilizers available commercially contain enough ammonium to nourish the plants properly and to quickly eliminate any ammonium deficiency. It is more difficult when there is an excess of nitrogenous compounds (see Cryptocoryne rot, page 53). Here as a rule the only remedy is a basic improvement of the aquarium milieu.

The concentration of the different nitrogen compounds is measured with commercially available test reagents.

Phosphorus

Phosphorus is a problematical plant nutrient in the aquarium. It is not taken up as

a pure element but as phosphate. Phosphate plays an important role in photosynthesis. Phosphate deficiency will hinder the manufacture of oxygen by slowing photosynthesis; in the aquarium this does not happen, however, since the plants can still take up scant traces and make use of them. But an excess of phosphate can easily occur because of the remnants of fish food. It leads to plant damage and — especially in the presence of excess nitrate — to the growth of algae.
Care: Through regular change of part of the water remove at least a portion of this residue.

Potassium, sodium

Potassium and sodium are usually present at low concentrations in our water supply. There is usually enough sodium content for the requirements of the tropical plants, but on the other hand there is often a potassium deficiency in many aquariums. Lack of potassium hinders photosynthesis and therefore damages the whole aquarium milieu.
Care: Fertilize. Good fertilizers contain potassium in sufficient amounts.

Trace elements

Iron is the most important trace element for the aquarium plants. It is a component of the enzyme that helps in the synthesis of chlorophyll. Iron deficiency leads to chlorosis (see page 53). In the wild, many aquatic plants grow in places where the iron-rich groundwater is exuded from the banks or bed of the stream. Groundwater also tends to be rich in other trace elements (like manganese, copper, zinc, tin, boron, and molybdenum). The plants grow thicker and larger the closer they are to the source of the nutrient. This water contains the iron and the other trace elements in a form that can easily be taken up by plants. But if the trace elements occur in oxygen-rich fast-flowing water, some of the trace elements may bind with the oxygen and precipitate, which is to say they become insoluble and are no longer useful to plants.
Care: Fertilize. So that the iron and the other trace elements are not precipitated out of the water, they are supplied in the aquatic-plant fertilizers as so-called chelates, which are synthetic organic acids that maintain all the trace elements over a long period in the form in which they can be utilized by the plants. Iron-rich slow-release fertilizers do for the aquarium floor what the seepage of groundwater does for the beds of tropical streams.

Besides the trace elements many aquatic plant fertilizers contain the other nutrients, such as ammonium and potassium. But pet stores also carry preparations that contain only the whole trace-element complex. With this you fertilize not just after each change of water but also more frequently with a few drops to keep the supply of these important nutrients at a constant level. Follow the directions on the bottle of trace element mix. You may want to determine the amount you need for your aquarium by measuring the iron, but test kits for this purpose are not always readily available.

Technology in the Planted Aquarium

Avoiding Electrical Accidents

Though electrical accidents with an aquarium very seldom occur, you should take all possible precautions against them.

Heating: Make sure when buying thermostatically controlled heaters, thermofilters, heating cables, and heating pads that the equipment you choose carries the UL approval notice. Thermostatically controlled heaters should be so installed in the aquarium that the cap with the regulating screw sticks up well above the water surface.

Lamps: Aquarium lamps and aquarium covers with built-in lamps have moisture-proof sockets and are waterproofed against splashes. Look for the UL approval notice.

Filter: Install and operate the filter according to the manufacturer's instructions. These days all electrical and moisture-sensitive parts are waterproofed with plastic resins.

Safety precautions

Installation of an electronic monitoring device is strongly recommended. Connected between the wall socket and the electrical equipment, it interrupts the current as soon as there is a failure in the equipment or the wiring. This monitor has four plugs so that it can be connected to all the electrical equipment in the aquarium. A circuit breaker functions the same way; it must be installed in a fusebox by an electrician. Aquariums should not be grounded. Make sure that all electrical equipment carries the UL approval notice.

Lighting

Light is the most important prerequisite for good growth of plants, for they use it as a source of energy to maintain their metabolism. Tropical plants will not flourish in natural daylight in northern regions. In summer it is too bright and too warm, and too many algae develop. In winter the light is too weak, and the plants languish. Artificial light is absolutely essential.

Duration of lighting period: The continual increase and decrease of the length of the day during the course of the year in our latitude does not agree with tropical plants. The majority of our aquarium plants originate in subtropical or equatorial areas, in which the day is between 12 and 14 hours long throughout the year. Therefore you must see to it that the aquarium day is as long as a tropical day. Connect the aquarium lamps to a timer that turns the light on and off automatically, so the aquarium is illuminated for 12 to 14 hours.

Light intensity: The plants have adapted to the light conditions in their habitat over millions of years; tropical plants are therefore very light-hungry.

A rule of thumb for the illumination of aquariums is: 0.4 to 0.7 watts per quart (1 L) of water, simplified as about 1 watt per 2 quarts (2 L). This turns out to be true for fluorescent tubes with the daylight spectrum; high-efficiency tubes have a light yield about 30 percent higher, and halogen and mercury-vapor lamps are also much brighter. (Bear the calculation in mind.) The wattages given in the plant descriptions (see page 56) relate to normal daylight tubes. More light is absorbed the more strongly the water is colored (the most strongly by peat filtering or addition of peat preparations). It is also important to know that the amount of light is diminished more the deeper the light penetrates into the water. Therefore you should double the light strength for every 4 inches (10 cm) of water to achieve the same plant growth in a high aquarium as in a shallow one. If you choose a tank approximately as deep as it is wide, you may find it difficult to mount large batteries of fluorescent lights over it. In that case you should try to obtain halogen or mercury-vapor lamps (see below), which are ideal for deep tanks!

Light color: Chlorophyll is activated most strongly by red and blue light. The long-wave length light of the red area of the spectrum promotes the vertical growth of the plants; the short-wavelength light of the blue, compact, sturdy growth. To the human eye, the fish and plants seem the most natural if they are illuminated by a light that approximates normal daylight. The aquarium light should be so chosen that the plants receive all the light colors in the proper mixture as well as in the correct light strength.

Fluorescent lights

Fluorescent lights are more economical and more readily available than all other types of lamps. You may need several tubes in different light colors.

Of the many different fluorescent tubes available, the most suitable are the "deluxe warm white," the Grolux, and the plant-lite tubes. In some areas the OSRAM Lumilux-Daylight tubes No. 11 and No. 21 may be available, and they, too, are suitable. Both the latter give off a lot of blue light; they should be used in combination with daylight bulbs, because otherwise the plants are stimulated to very powerful vertical growth. In addition they make some fish and plants appear in unnatural colors. For small aquariums, over which there is no room for a large light fixture with many different bulbs, deluxe warm white or Grolux-type bulbs alone will suffice. Fluorescent bulbs are the best lighting for shallow, wide aquariums, especially if they have sliding roofs. They can be suspended relatively close to the aquarium and will illuminate the whole tank evenly.

Mounting fluorescent tubes: You can get fluorescent bulbs in ready-made aquarium covers, in lamp housings that can be laid on the aquarium, or as hanging lamps. The hanging lamps are the most comfortable for the aquarist. The hanger can be shortened, giving you enough room to work in the lighted aquarium.

Changing the tubes: Fluorescent tubes deteriorate slowly, but still they have their limits. With a normal usage of 12 to 14 hours a day they have only 50 percent of their light strength after six months. Lamps over an aquarium in which the plants ought to grow especially well and in which are planted many cryptocorynes, which need very stable environmental conditions, must be changed after six months. This is especially true for the blue Grolux-type tubes. Delay in changing the fluorescent tubes may injure plants.

Note: A higher nitrate content raises the light requirement of the plants. In clean water they will thrive in less light; in water heavily burdened with nitrates the plant growth stagnates in spite of optimal light supply.

Mercury-vapor lamps

Mercury-vapor lamps are recommended for water depths of up to 24 inches (60 cm), particularly for tanks without roofs. However, mercury-vapor lamps are not commonly sold in pet stores; if you decide you want them, you may have to search around. They work like spotlights; therefore you can hang them directly over the plants that require a lot of light. Foreground plants like *Echinodorus tenellus, Echinodorus bolivianus, Lilaeopsis novae-zelandiae,* and other small swamp plants that in the wild need full sun often receive too little sun in the aquarium. They stand in the deepest part of the tank and have a whole column of light-absorbing water over them. The mercury-vapor lamps make it possible to target such light-seeking plants directly, while around them can be planted less light-loving and, at some distance from the light beam, even shade-loving varieties.

Halogen lamps

Halogen lamps use electricity more efficiently than mercury-vapor lamps. They have almost double the light output. Unfortunately they are very expensive to buy, and difficult to obtain in this country. Because they give off a great deal of heat, they warm the water of the aquarium too much if they are hung too close to it. However, halogen lamps are suitable for targeted illumination of especially light-loving plant groups. They also provide the best illumination of all for the aquarium that is more than 39 inches (1 m) high. Since their light spectrum is almost the same as daylight, all the light needs of the plants will be filled and the colors of the fish and the plants will appear natural. Like mercury vapor lamps, halogen lamps reach their full light strength slowly, in the course of the first five minutes after being turned on. This is very good for easily frightened fish.

Heating

Tropical plants thrive in temperature ranges of 70 to 86°F (21 to 30°C), but they grow best at about 73 to 81°F (23 to 27°C). Plants from subtropical zones can take cooler water; the most adaptable are cosmopolites like crystalwort (*Riccia fluitans*), which can stand temperatures of 54 to over 86°F (12 to over 30°C).

The plants, and the fish even more so, do not tolerate short-term temperature fluctuations well. The output of any aquarium

heater must thus be monitored and regulated by a thermostat. An aquarium thermostat holds the chosen temperature constant at about plus or minus 1.8°F (1°C).

Regulated heaters and thermofilters

A regulated heater is the most economical heater for the aquarium; it is a heating rod with a built-in thermostat. It is placed in the aquarium in a vertical position so that the cap with the regulating screw is above the water level.

The way floor heating works: Warm water circulates upward through the layers of fertilizer and pebbles, taking nourishment to the roots. Cooler water is sucked out the aquarium space down toward the floor. This way optimum water circulation occurs. (1 = thermostat; 2 = pebbles; 3 = slow-release fertilizer; 4 = heating pad; 5 = insulating layer.)

A thermofilter is practical and simple to manipulate. It consists of a filter with a built-in heating apparatus that is regulated by a thermostat. The water is thus heated while it is being filtered. These are more expensive and considerably less available than the rod-type heaters.

Floor heating

You can also equip your aquarium with a floor heater than will warm the gravel floor to 1.8 to 3.6°F (1 to 2°C) above the water temperature and thus produce a general circulation of water. Either heating cables or heating pads can be used. Ready-made systems are

uncommon in this country, so it will probably be necessary to build your own heater using the types of apparatus designed for warming reptile housing. The warmed water rises to the top and thereby the colder water is sucked down out of the aquarium, bringing a constant supply of nutrients and fresh water to the plant roots. The floor cannot rot, and noxious materials can be broken down by the bacteria that live in the gravel as well as by the filter bacteria. In the wild the water floor is usually somewhat colder than the water, but this type of circulation mimics the currents of the trickling springs (see trace elements, page 14), in which the plants grow best. This also avoids the plants getting "cold feet" in the event that the aquarium is in a room or area that is not heated well enough.
The heating cable is laid on the floor of the tank in coils and fastened to plastic strips or feet so that it doesn't rest on the glass. You can also make very good use of a heating cable in tanks in which plants are kept for propagating. Plants that especially need warmth can be set out in plant saucers or pots and wrapped with the heating cable.
The heating pad is placed outside the aquarium, underneath, and the bottom insulated with suitable material.

When you are using a heating pad the bottom material should not be too fine-grained or muddy! Impermeable material will not allow water to perfuse quickly enough, and heat build-up can result, which can crack the aquarium floor. Splits in the glass can also occur with a pad that is too powerful or one that is not installed according to instructions.
Care: Because the floor acts something like a filter, it will become dirty and stopped up after a time. Therefore you must clean it every year or so, or it will perfuse poorly and the water temperature will rise (especially

with the use of a heating pad under the stones and other large-surfaced decorative material). The plant roots will be damaged and the filter bacteria will die.

It is preferable not to heat the whole tank with a powerful heating pad, but to regulate a weak cable-heating system with a two-circuit thermostat, which on particularly cool days can turn on a supplementary heater. This suits the plants better and delays for a longer time the need to rearrange the aquarium.

Heat intensity

In unheated areas, for example in rooms that are heated only part of the time in winter or are heated minimally, the total aquarium heating output should amount to 1 watt per quart (liter) of water. If the tank is situated in a normally heated room of 68 to 73°F (20 to 23°C), an output of 0.3 to 0.5 watts per quart (liter) of water is enough; the tank needs only to be warmed a few degress above the surrounding temperature. Most aquariums will be warmed further by the illumination, especially if the lamps are hanging directly over the water.

Popular aquarium plants. ▷
Top left, *Echinodorus osiris*; top center *Aponogeton undulatus*; top right, *Aponogeton rigidifolius*. Center left, *Bolbitis heudelotii*; center center, underwater rose (*Samolus parviflorus*); center right, swordplant (*Echinodorus cordifolius*).
Bottom left, *Cryptocoryne wendtii*; bottom center, *Cryptocoryne x willsii*; bottom right, crystalwort, (*Riccia fluitans*).

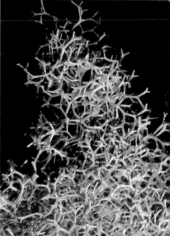

Technology in the Planted Aquarium

Filters and Aeration

Filters are needed primarily to filter out the excrement of the fish, the food remnants, and rotting plant bits that pollute the water and to transform them into materials that do not upset the balance of the aquarium. Dirty water is much more dangerous to fish than it is to plants. Therefore the needs of the fish should be given priority when the filter is chosen. Whether you opt for an inside or an outside filter and what brand you choose is not so important for the plants. Get advice from the pet store staff. Many Dutch aquariums (see page 43), in which only tiny fish swim in the abundant stands of plants, have no filter or have a small filter that is only running for a few hours per day.

Large filters that create a strong circulation with a centrifugal pump and spray the water back into the aquarium with pressure tubes are not for a plant aquarium. Also unsuitable are the stone diffusers driven by air pumps.

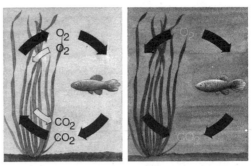

Oxygen (O_2) and carbon dioxide (CO_2) circulation. *By day* fish and plants consume O_2 in and expire CO_2; during photosynthesis, plants also take up CO_2 and produce O_2. *By night* (or weak light) fish and plants consume O_2 and expire CO_2. Photosynthesis cannot take place in the dark.

Both are only intended for "fish aquariums" in which few or no plants live. In a thickly planted tank the plants do indeed need a gentle or moderate current, but the water should not move too vigorously.

◁ Aquarium plants with red leaves.
Top, lotus lily (*Nymphaea lotus*), water wisteria (*Hygrophila difformis*).
Bottom, copper leaf (*Alteranthera reineckii*) among green water plants.

Buying and Planting

What To Consider When Choosing

For your aquarium to become a decorative focal point in your home, you need to assemble a functioning plant community. To achieve this, all types of plants should have approximately the same needs for water composition, temperature, and light intensity. Furthermore the maintenance requirements of the plants should be compatible with those of the fish you want to keep.

If you aren't one of those fish specialists who intends to raise one particular type of fish and so only installs one or a few kinds of plants in the aquarium as a spawning medium, you can compose your plantings from an aesthetic point of view and buy those kinds of plants whose effects will complement each other. Contrast finely feathered plants with large-leaved ones, bright green with dark green or red, rosette-formed plants with stem plants.

Tank size and plants

Choose plants according to the dimensions of your aquarium. Find out how big the plants grow (see plant descriptions, page 56), so that your plants need not be cut back constantly to fit the aquarium size. The plants only achieve their full beauty and their purifying and oxygen-producing characteristics if they can grow undisturbed for a long time and need not keep putting out new roots and healing wounds. For instance, stem plants that you cut back every few weeks and replant grow weaker and weaker as time goes on and eventually succumb.

For shallow tanks, tall stem plants, such as *Cabomba* (fanwort), the large *Hygrophila* species or *Heteranthera zosterfolia* (mud plantain), are not recommended. They must constantly be propped up and new groups formed from end cuttings every month (see page 35).

For small aquariums under 39 inches (1 m) long, plants that grow very large, such as *Echinodorus cordifolius* (swordplant) or tropical water lilies, are not suitable. Constant pruning would be necessary.

In large aquariums the size of the plants plays a role on aesthetic grounds. Here you need to be careful that the plants are not too small. A tank that is 79 inches (2 m) long and 27 inches (70 cm) high will not look very attractive if it is only planted with low-growing plants like *Echinodorus tenellus* (swordplant), *Samolus parviflorus* (underwater rose), or with low *Cryptocoryne* species.

Note: The descriptions and drawings of sixty attractive aquatic plants (see page 56) should help you make your plant choices. These provide details about size and appearance of plants as well as recommendations for their placement in the tank and also a number of tips.

Planting a brand-new aquarium

Experience teaches that it's unwise to plant the most demanding plants when you are starting a new aquarium. They often need a longer time to acclimate themselves and to grow. But water improvement can't wait that long, and algae can develop prolifically. If the algae plague becomes too bad, the fussy plants will die. It's better to plant the tank first with fast-growing, undemanding plants like *Ludwigia* and *Sagittaria*. They grow so quickly that the algae scarcely have a chance. When the aquarium has been "broken in" for a few months and the plants and fish are healthy, you can then exchange some of the easy plants for more demanding ones like species of *Cryptocorynes* and *Cambombas*. If

you introduce a new plant group into the tank every two to four weeks, there are always so many rooted and growing plants that the newcomer suffering from the stress of being transplanted will not be needed for water improvement. They even grow better in such a "broken-in" aquarium milieu.
Note: *Cryptocorynes* often will not grow at all in a newly established tank!

Plants not suitable for the aquarium

Now and again houseplants will be offered as aquarium plants — "underwater brome-liads," for example, or "underwater palms." These plants do not belong in the aquarium; they are land plants, whose structures are not suited for life in the water. Underwater a land plant can barely take up the nutrients and gases, and it can give off little or no oxygen. It vegetates in the water for a while, does nothing for the aquarium milieu, and takes the place of plants that are necessary for life until finally it dies. Furthermore, a dying plant is a dangerous source of rot in the aquarium.
Note: You can keep bromeliads, epiphytic cacti, *Fittonia*, and *Spathyphyllum wallisii* (a relative of the calla) in a paludarium (see page 47) without special care.

Buying Plants

These days some dealers no longer offer all plants with bare roots. Some recommended types are planted in little plastic pots with sides that are solid or of mesh. Cuttings may come bundled and with stems packed in a medium. If you have a choice between bare-root or potted plants, it is better to choose the potted types. They are hardier because they have not had to be dug up for transport from the grower to the dealer. The pots, which protect the roots and the stem, have kept the plants ready for planting in your aquarium without the danger of transplanting shock.

What to watch for when buying

Buy only healthy and — if possible — young plants:
● Healthy plants have erect leaves and stems and a strong color. Plants with many bent or browned leaves certainly will pull themselves together quickly with good care if their central leaves are healthy, but they are not recommended when you are establishing a new aquarium.
● Young plants adjust to the new circumstances in your aquarium more easily than old ones, for which the shock of transplanting is often so great that they lose a portion of their leaves.
● Pick off any leaves covered with algae.

Transporting the plants

Aquatic plants should be transported in a closed container or jar and take the plants home in water. In the winter the container must be wrapped in thick layers of newspaper or packed in a Styrofoam carton.

Care of the Plants Before Planting

Newly acquired plants must be cleaned before they are planted. So, when you get the plants home, lay them in a bowl of tepid water and open the package. Container plants should be laid in the water, pot and all. Cover them with a sheet of newspaper so that they don't dry out. The newspaper will absorb water and keep the portions of the plants that stick out of the water damp.

Buying and Planting

Cleaning the plants

Each plant should be taken out of the dish one at a time and cleaned:

Leaves and stem: Cut off portions that have dried out in transit. Dried-out leaves and stems of water plants die without fail. Crushed parts will never come back either, so they must be cut off, as must tattered or browned leaves and bent plant parts.

Roots: Healthy roots are pale and firm, dead ones brown and flabby. All dead ones should be cut off.

Note: Remove the pots from the container plants at this time. The root ball is not easy to remove from the solid containers. Strongly rooted plants are even hard to remove from the network pots. Try not to force them. It's better to cut these pots away from the roots piece by piece with a pair of sturdy shears so that the healthy roots are not damaged. Fiberglass or vermiculite must be carefully pulled out of the root ball of the stem plants.

Remove snail spawn?

Snail spawn may be found on some plants from the pet store and on many plants from a long-established aquarium.

You need not remove the snail spawn if you are only keeping fish and robust plants in your aquarium. Snails make themselves useful in the general aquarium because they consume food remnants and small algae.

You should remove the snail spawn if you are planning a tank primarily of plants, in which you want to keep fine-leaved, delicate varieties. Then carefully scratch the spawn from the plants. The red ramshorn snail (*Planorbis corneus*) loves the fine leaf tips of the *Limnophila* and *Cabomba,* and *Rotala macrandra* is a delicacy for all snails.

If you are using a slow-release fertilizer under the floor material (see page 33), it is better to scratch off all the spawn from newly bought plants. Certain varieties of snails will be very difficult to get out of the aquarium later.

If not removed, their rooting activities will mix the slow-release fertilizer with the upper pebble layer. Eventually, all the floor materials will be mixed up together, and a fertilizer containing large amounts of iron can color the water red.

Disinfecting the plants

Disinfecting the plants in a rose-colored solution of potassium permanganate or a weak alum solution before placing them in the aquarium is sometimes recommended to kill any pathogens, attached algae, or snail spawn that might be present. Delicate, thin-leaved plants can be injured by the disinfectant, however, so that sometimes part of the plant dies. It is much better to keep the aquarium milieu healthy through abundant planting, regular water change, and a fish population that is not too large so that the fish are strong and hardy and can withstand any pathogens.

Planting

If you are arranging a tank for the first time, fill the arranged and decorated aquarium about half or two thirds full of water before you begin planting. This way you will prevent the plants from becoming dried out and damaged while you are working. So as not to stir up the pebbles, lay a sheet of newspaper or brown paper in the tank, or put in a large plate. These will "steer" the stream of water when it pours in. The plants should only be planted when the water is warmed to at least 72°F (22°C); cold water — especially in winter — is too much of a shock for the plants.

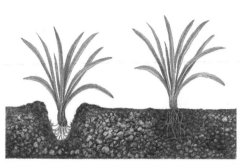

Proper planting: First place the plant deep in the planting hole (left), fill the hole with planting medium, and then draw the plant carefully upward so that the roots are properly settled (right).

Unrooted plants

Stem plants are usually unrooted. Plant them in groups but place each stem in a single hole. Then in case one of them rots, it can't infect the others. The new roots arise at the stem node. The plants should therefore be set at least two — and better four — nodes deep, so that they can develop enough roots. The leaves on the part of the stem underground should be removed (buried leaves rot!).

Fastening plants: Freshly set-out stem plants almost never rot, but if you have very expensive cuttings that you don't want to take any chances with, you can attach them to the floor with plant fasteners of glass or plastic (available in pet stores), without actually planting them. The new roots will then find their own way into the gorund. This method won't work if you are keeping very active or burrowing fish.

Rooted plants

You must shorten the roots of rooted stem plants and plants with ground-level leaf rosettes — no matter whether they were bought as container or bare-root plants. With a sharp knife or a sharp pair of shears cut off about half or two thirds of the roots. There should only be enough roots left to keep the plant standing and from swimming up. The pruning stimulates new roots. If the plant has a sturdy rootstock (rhizome or tough tuber), you can cut off almost all the roots. Be careful not to injure the roots stock while you are doing it. Then no broken place can die and rot. Until the development of new roots the plant can live on the stored reserves in the rootstock.

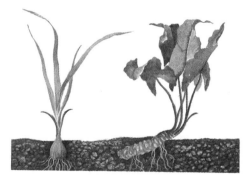

Proper planting of bulbs and rhizomes: Bury bulbs just deep enough so that the base of the leaves (crown) is still clearly visible (left). Set rhizomes at an angle; the crown must show above the ground (right).

Proper planting: Bore a hole in the ground with your finger, stick the plant as deeply into it as possible, fill the hole again, and press it in from the sides toward the center. The roots will usually be bent toward the surface by this procedure, but plants can't grow this way. To get the roots into the right position, now pull the plant carefully and gently upward until the neck of the root just appears over the surface of the ground. For *Saggitaria* and *Vallisneria* you should still see the upper 0.08 inches (2 mm) of the root. *Ceratopteris thalictroides* (water sprite) grows much faster if ½ to 1 inch (1 to 2 cm) of the root is showing above the ground.

Plants with rhizomes

Most of these plants must be set as deeply as possible, because only the node (stem node) of the rhizome will put out new roots. However, these plants tolerate just as poorly as all the others the burial of the crown, the place where the leaves sprout, in the pebbles. Therefore the rhizome should be planted at an angle, so the greater part of it lies in the ground and the yet the crown sticks up (see drawing page 25). This is especially important when planting cryptocorynes.

Planting tips

Many plants grow better if at planting you take into consideration the shape of the root ball as well as its special requirements. Thus the following tips and shortcuts:

Shallow-rooted plants — like the *Echinodorus* and *Aponogeton* species — should be set in broad, shallow depressions in which you can spread out the roots somewhat.

Deep-rooted plants — like *Cryptocorynes, Sagittarias,* and *Vallisnerias* — should be planted in small, deep holes. (Be careful not to dig out the slow-release fertilizer!)

Small foreground plants — like *Lilaeopsis novae-zelandiae* — which grow thickly matted in their plastic pots, can often not be separated. Simply open the package, prune the

roots where possible, and plant the whole thing like a single plant.

Especially delicate plants need special handling when being planted:

● *Aponogeton* tubers, which you buy during their resting phase, have no leaves. Therefore it is very important to place them in the ground correctly. The "eyes," from which the leaves grow, must be on the top side when they are planted, or the plant will not grow!

● *Anubia* species have such tender roots that it is better not to prune them at all. Simply lay the plant on the pebbles and anchor the rhizome with a stone or with a plant fastener. The young roots then find their own way into the ground. You can also bind the plant to a piece of wood or to a porous stone with plastic cord; it will root there. *Anubias barteri var. nana* is not so delicate.

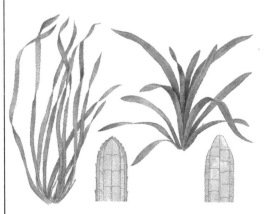

Vallisneria (left) and *Sagittaria* (right) are often confused; *Vallisneria* leaves have fine, saw-toothed margins, and the veins all run together at the tips of the leaves. *Sagittaria* leaves are smooth; the side veins end at the margins well before the tips of the leaves.

• *Microsorium (Polypodium) pteropus* and *Bolbitis heudelotii* grow better on swamp pine and lava than in the ground. When you plant them, the rhizomes (as with *Anubias*) should not be buried.

• Water lilies (*Nuphar* and *Nymphaea*) should be placed on the pebbles and fastened (like *Anubias*, see above).

• The banana roots of the banana plant (*Nymphoides aquatica*) are set into the ground to one quarter of their length, at most, or are only laid on it and fastened with plant clips. They are so delicate that they can be injured, get rotten spots, and ultimately die if you plant them between sharp pebbles.

• *Crinum* species are also sensitive to pressure and sharp little stones. They are best planted wrapped in peat moss fibers. The root area of the bulb should not be covered by the fibers, so that freshly sprouting roots will not be impeded.

• Do not prune the roots of the floating plants. Lay the plants beside one another on the surface of the water. If they have gotten tangled with each other in transit or if the roots have become stuck to the upper surface, you need only to submerge them in the water a few times. They will untangle themselves on their own and float back to the surface in the proper position.

Decorating the Aquarium

The general aquarium literature gives a great deal of information about decoration materials and their use in the aquarium. The following are only a few important points:

Stones (basalt, granite, lava, northern schist, and so forth) must be chalk-free! Brown stones contrast especially well with plants.

Swamp pine (available in pet stores), which does not rot in the aquarium, should be cleaned and actually boiled before you introduce it into the tank. The roots must be soaked until they are saturated; otherwise they will float to the top.

Hiding places and spawning places are created by roots or by stones piled up to make caves or by boiled-out coconut shells.

Back and side walls should be decorated with: painted paper or Styrofoam fastened to the outside walls, or stone walls inside the aquarium (stones set in cement, and the finished wall allowed to soak for about two weeks to wash out all the excess alkali), cork walls (cork bark boiled, dried, and glued to hard PVC plates), or polyurethane plates that have been shaped by pulling. Plastic back walls can also be bought. These wall decorations can also be used in a paludarium (see page 47). All animals feel better if their environment is not open on all sides.

The bottom material must be chalk-free. You can use quartz gravel in a grain size of 2 to 3 mm. Finer gravel may interfere with the circulation if there is bottom heat and easily lead to rot. Too much mulm falls into the spaces between the larger pebbles, and in time it thickens too. For best plant growth, use one of the iron-rich slow-release fertilizers (available commercially) under the gravel. Follow the manufacturer's instructions. The slow-release fertilizer is necessary because with good light the plants will grow quickly and require much nourishment. The pebbles should be brown or colored; bright gray reflects the light too strongly and this disturbs the fish.

Building terraces: Upright glass strips fastened to the tank floor and the side walls with silicone rubber, the front concealed with stones, swamp pine, or cork (glued on), blend neatly with the back wall. Terrace building stones or peat titles for wall building are available in the pet stores. Then, in the different areas that are created by the terrace, you can use different kinds of planting mediums for plants with varying requirements.

Algae-eating fish: Install some algae-eating fish in the newly established tank as quickly as possible (don't feed them for two weeks!); otherwise the algae will grow faster than the plants. Siamese flying fox (*Epalzeorhynchus siamensis*) and bristle-mouth or blue-chin catfish (*Ancistrus dolichopterus*) work best, but many other sucker-mouth armored catfish (*Otocinclus, Panaque, Hypostomus, Rhineloricaria* and *Farlowella* species) and all live-bearing killifish are also good algae scourers.

Top left, *Microsorium (Polypodium) pteropus* on cork ▷ bark; top right, water pennywort (*Hydrocotyle leucocephala*).
Bottom: Aquarium with asiatic plants and various barb species. Back, left, ambulia (*Limnophila sessiliflora*); back center, tape grass (*Vallisneria spiralis*); front left, water wisteria (*Hygrophila difformis*); front right, *Cryptocoryne affinis*.

Care and Propagation of Plants

Care of Plants

Aquariums that are organized chiefly for the care of plants make scarcely any more work than those planted or unplanted tanks in which the arrangements are tailored to the requirements of the fish.

Daily: The fish must be fed.

Weekly: You should clean the viewing wall and the top (if there is one) with a sponge or a good glass-cleaner from the pet store. Nibbled or drying leaves and stems should be removed. Mulm the fish have stirred up, which consists of the fallen finely feathered leaves of *Cabomba* or *Limnophila* species, is carefully removed.

Stem plants

Prune stem plants as soon as they reach the water surface. You can let them grow further and stream along the upper surface because they then become more luxuriant and also branch. But as soon as they take too much light away from the bottom plants, they must be cut back:

• With plants that branch profusely after pruning (like *Hygrophila* species), you can leave the rooted bottom end of the stem in place and let it sprout again.

◁ Top left, hornwort (*Ceratophyllum demersum*); top center, tape grass (*Vallisneria spiralis*); top right, *Shinnersia rivularis*.
Center left, *Vallisnerai gigantea*; center center, *Cabomba piauhyensis*; center right, *Sagittaria subulata*.
Bottom left, waterweed (*Egeria densa*); bottom center, *Limnophila sessiliflora*; bottom right, water lettuce (*Pistia stratiotes*).

• Other species (like *Cabomba*) branch very little after being cut back, and the new growth remains small and weak. Therefore you should remove the whole plant group, cut off any shoots that are over 8 inches (20 cm) long for cuttings, and plant a new group of these end cuttings. The lower portion can be thrown away.

Rosette plants

From time to time the old leaves or the plant stock of rosette plants need to be thinned out. As with all care procedures, you must work carefully so as to be sure that the plants retain their natural growth form and the appearance of the plant is not impaired.

Plants with very large growth habits: Swordplants (*Echinodorus cordifolius*), the water lilies (*Nymphaea* and *Nuphar*) and the *Lagenandra* species must have their growth controlled in most terrariums. As soon as they become too large, pick off the large outer leaves; in addition, make a cut with a sharp knife all around the roots, some 6 inches (15 cm) away form the leaf crown. The plant will then grow new roots and for the time being will not grow further; the water lilies do not grow any floating leaves. If the *Nymphaea* or *Nuphar* species are to bloom, you should leave them three or five floating leaves. If you don't value the blooms, you can cut off the floating leaves as soon as they appear, so that they do not take away light from the underwater plants.

Plants producing runners: *Sagittaria* and *Vallisneria,* for example, or grassy foreground plants like *Echinodorus tenellus* must be thinned now and again. Otherwise, in very thick grassy clumps in strong light, so many algae develop that the fish can't eat them anymore and they cannot even be removed by human intervention. As a pre-cautionary measure periodically remove the weaker young plants or even sometimes take out an old plant so that the clump always stays young. Because the shoots don't stand alone — on the contrary whole "chains" develop (see drawing page 16) — usually you must take out several at one time. This leaves large holes in the planting, so you may need to replant some of the removed ones.

You must work very carefully in removing old plants. Especially with the small *Echinodorus* species, it can happen that broken roots or pieces of root remain in the ground, rot, and affect the young plants around them. Ugly holes in the "grasses" will be the result. Very matted clumps are usually better removed entirely and the strongest young plants picked out and replanted anew. (*Cryptocorynes* should be treated this way.)

Plants with resting periods: Among aquarium plants it is mostly the relatives of the genus *Aponogeton* that need a resting period. These species possess a tuber of stored nutrients. *Aponogeton* tubers sprout quickly after being planted and grow and bloom very lushly in favorable circumstances, but after about eight months they enter their resting period and gradually lose all their leaves: they go dormant. One can simply leave the tubers in the aquarium; after several weeks they usually sprout again.

In case no new leaves appear after two months, dig them up and let them lie on the ground for a few weeks. After replanting they put out new shoots. The fish should not be allowed to eat the tubers under any circumstances.

Many *Aponogeton* species, however, are exhausted by the constant warmth of the tropical aquarium and grow weaker from year to year. Most manage better if you plant them in a shallow saucer that you can take out of the tank as soon as the plants go dormant. Store them for two to three months in a cooler aquarium, where the plants are kept at temperatures up to 61°F (16°C) and in little light. After they are returned to the tropical aquarium, they sprout readily at temperatures of over 68°F (20°C).

Changing the Water

If only a few fish live in your tank, it is usually enough to siphon off a fifth, at most a third, of all the aquarium water every two weeks and to replace it with fresh water. But the more and the larger the fish and the fewer plants you have, the more often the water should be changed.

Siphoning off the water: You need a 5-foot (1.5-meter) long hose with a diameter of ½ to 1 inch (1.5 to 2 cm) and a large pail. If more than 10 quarts (10 liters) of water are going to be changed, it may be necessary to have several pails ready for the siphoned-off water so that you won't have to stop in the middle. To siphon, place the end of the tube in the aquarium and suck strongly on the other end with your mouth. The water will thus be lifted over the edge of the container and then will run down the tube by itself into the pail that is standing ready. Be careful that the pail doesn't overflow! It's possible to get a little aquarium water in your mouth this way. If you want to avoid this, completely fill the hose at the water faucet, hold your thumb over the ends, and carry the full hose to the aquarium. Then hold one end in the aquarium and the other in the pail and take away your thumbs. The water should run.

With the hose end that is in the aquarium, move around the floor of the tank as if with a vacuum cleaner and take up the mulm that

Care and Propagation of Plants

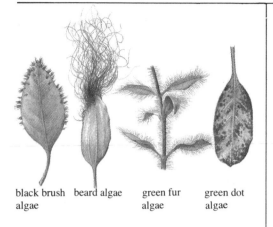

black brush algae   beard algae   green fur algae   green dot algae

Red algae and green algae that can appear in the aquarium (Control of algae, page 54).

has built up from the remains of food, excrement of the fish, and so forth. Be careful not to suck up too much gravel!

Note: Thoroughly remove mulm from stands of *Cryptocoryne*. If tender root tips are sticking up, the ground is coagulated. In that event, cultivate the ground and thin stands of plants.

Refilling the tank: Pour in the fresh water slowly so that the gravel and the mulm are not stirred up.

Fertilizing the Plants

How often you fertilize your plants and what you use depends on the number of plants, the light intensity, the water temperature, the species and number of fish (fertilizer production), and the fertilizing equipment you chose when you set up your aquarium.

Slow-release fertilizers are laid down with the floor material when the aquarium is established (follow the manufacturer's instructions). Additional fertilizing with a liquid iron-rich fertilizer is done after each partial change of water.

Liquid fertilizers can also be used alone in the aquarium without a slow-release fertilizer in the floor material. You fertilize for the first time when you set up the aquarium, then after each partial change of water. Follow the instructions on the package carefully, because the dosage so different for various products.

Proper fertilizing

No matter what fertilizer you use, observe the following ground rules:

● Use only a commercial product designed for aquarium plants! Fertilizers intended for land plants usually contain nitrogen in the form of nitrates that the water plants can't use or that may even harm them. Nitrates may injure fish in any case!

● Fertilize moderately but regularly. Aquarium plants grow much better this way than if they receive large doses of fertilizer at long intervals.

● Fertilize *after* each partial water change (quantity according to instructions on package). In the event that you use a water purification additive (it precipitates chemicals out of the water system), do the fertilizing one to two days later.

● Trace elements should be added according to package directions.

CO_2 fertilization

Carbon dioxide (CO_2) is an important nutrient. Even with optimal lighting, fertilization, and ground warmth, growth stops if the plants don't get enough CO_2. The use of supplemental CO_2 fertilization may be necessary for tanks with many plants. If you have found a mechanical system, install it and operate it according to the manufacturer's instructions.

How Water Plants Reproduce

There are two types of reproduction in plants.
● Sexual reproduction through seeds (as with flowering plants) or spores (as with ferns and mosses).
● Vegetative (asexual) reproduction through runners (stolons) or shoots or division of the parent plants.

In nature, many of our aquarium plants grow in water with seasonally lower water level or in swamps. They use both modes of reproduction. In the damp seasons, when they are underwater, they spread vegetatively by means of shoots, and they bloom and fruit if the water level sinks and they must grow emersed. The way plants in the aquarium or the paludarium reproduce is described in the plant descriptions that begin on page 56, under the heading Propagation.

Vegetative Reproduction

Both with the flowering plants — rosette and stem plants — and with the ferns and mosses, vegetative reproduction in the aquarium is far simpler and more successful than the sowing of seeds (sexual reproduction). Therefore most of our aquarium plants are propagated vegetatively. There are a number of ways to do this. Besides propagation through shoots and adventitious plants (see page 35), which works in nature the same way it works in the aquarium, you can get young plants from parts of older plants if you intervene in the growth process intelligently.

Shoots, runners

Shoots are young plants that develop at the end of a runner some distance from the parent plant. Each runner develops from a leaf axis of the old plant and corresponds to a side branch. Therefore shoots are only to be found in plants with extended stem axes — for example, *Vallisneria, Sagittaria,* the grassy *Echinodorus* species, and *Cryptocoryne.* Most of these develop long chains of young plants. Propagation from shoots is without problems if you observe the following:
● Don't cut shoots too soon. They should be at least a third, and better half, as large as the old plant before you take them off and should be planted in their new location with shortened roots. Otherwise they will grow badly and will keep being pulled out by the fish.
● If possible, leave some shoots standing by the parent plant; plant groups usually look more attractive than single plants.
● With species that increase prolifically by means of runners, like *Vallisneria* or the smaller *Echinodorus* species, thin the clumps often so that they don't mat. You can replant the strongest of the young plants in another location.
● Most sensitive are the runners of the cryptocorynes. They may only be cut if the new plant is almost as large as the parent plant. (Cryptocorynes tolerate transplanting very badly.)

Shoots and runners of floating plants:
Among the floating plants there are many varieties that put out runners. *Eichornia crassipes* (water hyacinth), *Pistia stratiotes* (water lettuce), and the floating ferns *Ceratopteris pteridoides* (water sprite) and *Salvinia auriculata* put out a great many runners when growing conditions are good. The runners are usually shorter-lived than those of plants that root in the ground. The connec-

Care and Propagation of Plants

Propagation of *Echinodorus* by runners: Cut the runners when the young plant is half as large as the parent plant. The next runner in the chain will grow from the bud (gemma) at far right.

tion of the young plant to the parent plant deteriorates very quickly. You therefore don't need to prune them back. If the floating plants increase too much, you must thin them so that they don't take too much light away from the plants on the floor.

Adventitious plants

Adventitious plants are plants that arise from the parent plant itself. They develop in different places according to the individual plant species.

Microsorium (Polypodium) pteropus **and** *ceratopteris* **species:** These plants produce buds at the margins of the leaves from which the young plants develop. The new plants develop roots, but often they do not separate themselves from the parent plant but develop new adventitious plants of their own. Therefore a *Microsorium pteropus* can develop plants with several "stories."

Echinodorus **species:** In the larger types like *Echinodorus cordifolius, Echinodorus bleheri,* or *Echinodorus osiris,* the adventitious

plants develop at the whorls of the submerged flower stalk.

Aponogeton **species:** In *Aponogeton undulatus* and *Aponogeton stachyosporus* the adventitious plant grows like a flower.

Hygrophila **species:** In the large species like *Hygrophila difformis* or *Hygrophila polysperma* one or more buds appear at the base of individual leaves that one allows to float on the water surface; the young plants develop from these buds.

Propagation by means of adventitious plants: Adventitious plants must not be separated from the parent plant too soon. Before you remove them and plant them they should have developed at least eight leaves and strong roots. Young *Aponogeton* plants must also have a little tuber.

Adventitious plants that develop on the pedicel need not necessarily be separated. Just bend the stalk with its new growth to the floor and fasten it there with a stone or a plant clamp. The young plants will take root by themselves and after a while, when they are strong enough, they can be cut off.

Adventitious plants on the edges of floating ferns do not have to be separated. Simply let them grow and thin them out of the floating plant cover only if they become too thick.

Cuttings

Stem plants — that is, plants with extended stems — can be propagated by means of cuttings. A cutting is a section of stalk (stem and leaves) that is placed in the ground and which then grows roots at the stem node. The side branches of a stem plant can be used as cuttings or the whole plant can be cut into separate pieces. The upper part is called an end cutting, the others stem cuttings or side shoots.

Care and Propagation of Plants

Propagation by means of cuttings: Each cutting should be about 6 to 8 inches (15 to 20 cm) long and should have at least three, and better four, nodes. Cuttings should be made with sharp shears or a sharp knife (don't crush them!). At least two stem nodes should be covered with earth so that they can develop enough new roots (see planting of unrooted plants, page 25).

End cuttings and side shoots grow more quickly than stem cuttings because they have retained their vegetative cones. They also look more attractive to start with than the stem cuttings, which must first develop a new vegetative cone at the leaf axis. You can easily take cuttings of undemanding plants like *Ludwigia,* the *Hygrophila* species and *Heteranthera zosterifolia* (mud plantain). You cut the stems into small pieces that have only one or two stem nodes, retain the upper leaf pair (or only one), and stick it into the ground at an angle. This short cutting roots itself and, at a leaf node, puts out a bud from which a side shoot will eventually grow.

Peculiarities of free floating plants: Plants that can take up all their nutrients through leaves and stems need not be planted. Among these are the waterweeds (*Egeria, Elodea*) and the hornworts (*Ceratophyllum*). They can be propagated by means of many branching side shoots and even through 2-inch (5-cm) stem cuttings, which are merely allowed to float on the water surface. (Older parts that become glassy-looking should be removed.)

How not to treat cuttings: All cuttings will also root if you don't plant them but allow them to float on the surface of the water. At first glance this seems to be an easy way to proceed. But because each plant grows toward the light, the floating pieces of stem works its way to the surface and grows out of it there. Later, when you come to plant it, the cutting is bowed. The bend in the stem will never become straight again; the plant will grow toward the light again when it is planted, thus developing a second bend in the opposite direction. Such crooked plants don't look very attractive.

If you decide to use this method all the same, plant the crooked cutting with its bend toward the floor so that is can grow more vertical.

Dividing whole plants

Plants with rosette-formed leaf crowns and a shortened stem axis are usually used in the aquarium as single plants. To increase them you can divide the whole plant.
● Cut the plant through the middle with a sharp knife, so that the crown, the vegetative cone, is cut into two pieces.
● Prune the roots.
● Remove some of the leaves so that the leaf mass is in proper proportion to the size of the root ball. Either pluck off all the old, large leaves and leave only the young, small leaves on the plant, or cut back every old leaf by one half or one third.
● Plant both parts.

Maintenance note: It takes a long time for a divided plant to restore itself again, put out new shoots, and resume its natural growth form. Therefore you should plant divided single plants in an extra tank and give them the best possible care so that they don't succumb to shock or begin to rot at the cut place.

Dividing rosette plants in the root area

Some plants have rhizomes, bulbs, or tubers, which serve them as food storage in times of need (for example during dry spells).

Rhizome division: Because rhizomes are modified stems, they branch, and young

Care and Propagation of Plants

Propagation of cryptocorynes: Cut through the rhizome between the individual plants with a very sharp knife. The young plants should be almost as large as the parent plants.

plants grow from their vegetative cones. The branching of a rhizome is thus similar to that of a side shoot. To propagate, you can cut off the young plants or divide the old rhizome. Separating young plants: As soon as the young plant has about ten leaves of its own, you can separate its rhizome from the parent plant. Proceed as follows:

● Carefully lay aside the roots of the parent plant and with a very sharp knife — and without crushing — cut off the rhizome as close as possible to the parent plant.

● Carefully pull out the young plant and cover the roots of the parent plant with the ground material again.

● Then plant the young plant (see plants with rhizomes, page 26). Dividing old rhizomes: You can also use the old part of the rhizome that no longer possesses leaves for propagation.

● Cut off a rhizome about 2 inches (5 cm) from the leaf crown with a sharp knife and plant the leafed part in fresh ground. After a clean cut, a protective callus quickly forms

and the plants continue to grow, as soon as they have overcome the shock of transplanting.

● Divide the unleafed part into several pieces — for *Nymphaea* and *Nuphar* species about 4 inches (10 cm) long, for *Echinodorus* species 1 to 2 inches (3 to 5 cm) long, and for *Cryptocoryne* species about 2 inches (5 cm) long.

● Cut off the roots entirely and place the rhizomes in a tank of lukewarm water (about 72°F [22°C]). After some time a couple of buds will begin to appear. When new roots have developed on the rhizome, you can replant it in the aquarium.

Rhizome division in ferns: With the ferns *Bolbitis heudelotii* and *Microsorium (Polypodium) pteropus* cut off the rear rhizome pieces that no longer bear leaves but are still green. The pieces of rhizome should be about 2 inches (5 cm) long. Bind them to wood or stone. As soon as they are rooted, they will branch and put out new leaves.

Tuber division: You can divide the tubers of the *Aponogeton* species with a sharp knife during their resting stage. Each cut piece must retain one or more "eyes," from which the new plants will grow. Division of *Aponogeton* species is not really recommended because the cut surface has a strong tendency to rot. Aponogetons are propagated much more easily and safely by seeding or by adventitious plants.

Propagation by bulblets: The bulbs of the *Crinum* species are not divided. They put out bulblets (bulbils). When you want to separate the young plants, you must dig up the parent bulb and take off the bulblets. The leaves of the young plant should be more than half as long as those of the parent plant. Then the young bulb is about one third to one half as large as the old one and can be carefully loosened and wrapped in peat fibers and planted again.

Tissue culture

Today it is even possible to raise aquarium plants like orchids by tissue culture, in which small plant pieces are cut off and grow to complete plants in petri dishes or test-tubes filled with growing medium and nutrients. This is particularly successful with cryptocorynes. If this kind of vegetative reproduction works, you get a large number of young plants in a short time. They are all genetically the same, since they all came from one parent plant. Nevertheless, tissue culture is one of the most difficult undertakings in the aquarium field, for the work with sterile dishes, growing media, plant substrates, and so forth, cannot be mastered, even by a very interested layperson, at the first attempt. Those interested can learn more about it in the scientific literature and in magazines about orchid growing and raising.

Sexual Reproduction

The sexual reproduction of aquarium plants is much more demanding than vegetative reproduction. It belongs to "college-level" water-plant gardening, so to speak. For the sowing and raising of young plants to be successful, many holding and propagating aquariums are necessary for submersed and emersed culture. And it can still happen that the efforts of the gardener are not crowned with success. Seedlings of the delicate plants often don't thrive well, even with the best possible care. One must assume that certain nutrients or trace elements that the plants have at their disposal in free nature are available in too little quantity in our aquarium

water, in spite of the best fertilization. It may also be that some kind of waste or toxic product that is not present in natural, free-flowing water affects the seedlings. For those plant fanciers who want to try sexual propagation, the following is a short introduction.

Which plants bloom?

Whether our aquarium plants bloom depends not only on the type of plant but also on its living conditions.

In all aquariums, even those with covers, plants that live submerged all year around bloom comparatively easily, for example the water lilies (*Nuphar, Nymphaea*), *Vallisneria,* the waterweed species (*Egeria, Elodea*) and the *Aponogeton* species.

In aquariums without covers, most *Echinodorus* species and almost all stem plants such as lobelia, limnophila, or hygrophila come into flower.

In paludariums the cryptocorynes and the anubias will bloom. These plants can also be brought to bloom regularly in a makeshift paludarium: The plants are placed in their own tank that is only filled 0.8 to 1.6 inches (2 to 4 cm) high with water. It must be heated gently and tightly covered so that the plants

Sample paludariums for fish and tropical frogs. ▷
Emergent plants: top left, *Ficus pumila*; center left, *Spathyphyllum wallisii*; center, *Vriesia splendens*; right above, *Schefflera actinophylla*; right, behind, *Maranta leuconeura* "Fascinator."
Submersed plants: center, water milfoil (*Myriophyllum spec.*); at right, *Cryptocoryne affinis*.

are in damp air constantly. The floor can be covered with sphagnum moss (see photograph page 40); bottom heat is recommended. After the blooming period they can go back into the aquarium. The plants best tolerate the change between being submersed and emersed and the reverse if they are potted (in pots filled with nourishing ground medium).

Pollination

In the aquarium the insects and wind that take care of pollination in nature are lacking, so the gardener must carry the pollen from plant to plant himself. For small, delicate flowers this is done with a fine watercolor brush (marten fur), for the larger ones with a swab of cotton, and for the largest ones simply with a finger. In general, only species of *Aponogeton* regularly produce viable seeds; seed production by other species is sporadic.

Most plants cannot be pollinated with their own pollen. In most bisexual flowers the male and female sex cells usually mature at different times so that self-pollination is ruled out. Such flowers are called self-sterile. Plants in which the pollen and the ovules mature at the same time are called self-fertile; they can be pollinated with their own pollen.

Sowing

Seeds must be collected in the aquarium before they fall into the water and are sucked into the filter or are eaten by the fish. If it is not possible to oversee the plants so that you can harvest the ripe fruit or the seeds, it is recommended that you wrap the flower cluster in gauze and fasten it. The seeds will then fall into the gauze bag. It isn't known how long the seeds of most aquarium plants remain capable of germination. Therefore they should be sown as soon as possible after they are harvested. Most will not germinate in deep water. Proceed with the sowing as follows:

- Fill a shallow dish with a sand-loam mixture or sand-loam-peat mixture.
- Lightly press the seeds into the mixture at about ½ inch (1 cm) intervals or just lay them on the mixture and cover with a light layer of sand. Very small seeds can just be pressed in with the hand.
- Place the seed saucer either in a well-covered aquarium with a very shallow water level (up to 1½ inches [4 cm]), or in a large tank let it float just under the water surface. You can also suspend it under the water surface with a plastic holder, place it on a big pile of stones, or fasten it to the upper part of the back wall.

Lower the seed dish under the water very carefully so that the water streaming in doesn't wash out the seeds.

◁ Maintenance of emergent water and swamp plants.
Top: small paludarium with decorative plants.
Bottom: Plant dishes with swamp and water plants—for example, water lettuce (left and right), small water lilies, and maidenhair grass.

Care and Propagation of Plants

• If the seeds germinate, they must be sunk deeper into the aquarium as they grow.
Other sowing methods: You can also place a little plastic tank on the windowsill over a radiator or stand it on the stable cover of an aquarium, so that it will be warmed from underneath. Mix commercial aquarium soil (no concentrates) with coarse sand (half the volume), fill with 2 to 4 inches (5 to 10 cm) of water, and carefully press the seeds into the ground. Raise the water level as soon as the young plants appear out of the water. Illuminate about 13 hours per day. Install red ramshorn snails to combat algae.

Plant Aquariums and Paludariums

The Dutch Plant Aquarium

A Dutch aquarium is an underwater garden in which plants with the same needs for light, temperature, water composition, and fertilizer are planted and their contrasting shapes and colors are so arranged that a harmonious total effect of decoration and planting results. The requirements of the plants are the first consideration, not those of the fish. Fish are therefore chosen according to the plants, and not the plants according to the fish, as in a fish aquarium.

Plant aquariums have long been a specialty of the Dutch aquarists, who live in an area with soft- to medium-hard, slightly acidic water, which is best suited to the successful maintenance of many tropical plants. Since the development of ion-exchangers, CO_2-fertilizing devices, and iron-rich water-plant fertilizers, it has become possible for any lover of water plants to arrange a flourishing underwater world for himself, even if he lives in an area with very limey, hard water.

A well-planted Dutch aquarium is a fascinating eye-catcher in any living room, no matter whether it simply stands on a solid table with the technical equipment "hidden" behind houseplants, or whether you build it up with an arrangement of suitable materials so that the technical equipment cannot be seen at all. You can also use the tank as a room divider or install it as a wall decoration in a place that has been broken through the wall for the purpose. If you want to use houseplants in the arrangement of your Dutch aquarium, you must be sure that these plants also get enough light. If necessary you must also provide artificial light (fluorescent tubes or halogen lamps).

All the elements of decoration — wood, cork, stone, and even plastic — can be used. And for plants you can use almost anything you like that will produce an aesthetic effect. It's best to make a plan on paper first.

Arranging a small plant aquarium

The arrangement of tanks under 48 inches (1.2 m) in length should be planned particularly carefully. Small tanks quickly become busy and overburdened with too many decorations and plants.
- Decorate back and side walls from outside.
- Use only one terrace.
- Use only a few beautifully formed stones or bizarrely shaped roots.
- Plant seven to twelve different kinds of plants at most.

Planting suggestions for the small aquarium

Background: A group of one each of *Hygrophila difformis, Rotala rotundifolia* or *Ammannia gracilis, Hygrophila corymbosa* (red-brown) or *Heteranthera zosterifolia*, in shady places *Microsorium (Polypodium) pteropus*.

Middle ground: On the side, groups of *Rotala macrandra, Cabomba aquatica, Myriophyllum aquaticum*, in the middle groups of *Cryptocoryne wendtii* and *Didiplis (Peplis) diandra*.

Foreground: A solitary *Aponogeton crispus* growing on a lawn of *Echinodorus tenellus* or *Lilaeopsis novae-zelandiae*, at one side a group of *Cryptocoryne affinis*.

Arranging a large plant aquarium

A tank that is 72 inches (2 m) long, 18 inches (50 cm) wide, and 22 inches (55 cm) high can look this way:
- Back and side walls covered on inside with cork, stone, or plastic and planted here and

there with *Vesicularia dubyana* and *Microsorium (Polypodium) pteropus*.

● One to two terraces, the highest not more than 10 inches (25 cm) high, covered with swamp pine or the same material used for the back wall.

● Some colored stones that blend well with each other and the plants and/or swamp pine roots on the ground.

● Be sure when planting to leave a "see-through" to the terrace wall and the back wall so that the effect of depth is maintained and the beautiful materials are not covered up.

Planting suggestions for large tanks
Background (top terrace): Large groups of *Heteranthera zosterifolia, Rotala macrandra, Hygrophila difformis, Ammannia senegalensis,* and *Limnophila aquatica* or · *Limnophila sessiliflora* or a *Cabomba* species; added to this, some large-leaved plants such as *Echinodorus osiris, Echinodorus parviflorus, Echinodorus bleheri* or a larger cryptocoryne.
Middle ground (second highest terrace): *Cryptocoryne beckettii, Cryptocoryne griffithii* or *Cryptocoryne cordata;* added to this small bushes of *Didiplis (Peplis) diandra, Hemianthus micranthemoides, Lobelia cardinalis,* and some higher-growing groups of *Hygrophila corymbosa*. In between, place some solitary larger plants such as *Aponogeton crispus, Cryptocoryne pontederiifolia* or *Nymphaea lotus*.
Foreground: Grasslike plants such as *Echinodorus tennellus* or *Echinodorus quadricostatus var. xinguensis,* the small *Cryptocoryne x willisii* and the brown *Cryptocoryne wendtii* in one of their many forms. In between, some larger plants like a small group of the slender *Cryptocoryne balansae,* an *Aponogeton ulvaceus* or an *Aponogeton undulatus*.

Floating plants: Only in small quantities or better not used at all, since they take away too much light from the plants rooted on the bottom.

Fish for the Dutch aquarium

The fish for a plant aquarium should not be too large and not too lively. Of course they should not be plant eaters. Fish species that root in the ground or make trenches for spawn are also not recommended. You can keep the following fish in a planted aquarium without difficulty:

All small-to-medium-sized characin species like the cardinal tetra *(Paracheirodon axelrodi),* the common neon tetra *(Paracheirodon innesi),* the black tetra *(Gymnocorymbus ternetzi),* all *Hemigrammus* species like the glowlight tetra *(Hemigrammus erythrozonus)* and the beacon fish or head-and-tail-light tetra *(Hemigrammus ocellifer),* the *Hyphessobrycon* species like the blood characin *(H. callistus),* the bleeding heart tetra *(H. erythrostigma),* and the black neon *(H. herbertaxelrodi).* In addition all species of the hatchetfish like *Carnegiella strigata* and *Gasteropelecus maculatus,* all characins of the genera *Nannostomus* and *Nematobrycon,* the penguin fish *(Thayeria boehlkei),* and the splash tetra *(Copella arnoldi).*
Of the barbs and small barbs, the zebra fish of the genera *Danio* and *Brachydanio* are suitable, as are the black ruby barb *(Barbus nigrofasciatus),* the checkered barb *(Barbus oligolepsis),* the dotted barb *(Barbus ticto)* and Cuming's barb *(Barbus cumingii)* as well as all the barbs of the genus *Rasbora.*
All species of guppies *(Poeciliidae)* if the water is not too soft (not less than 12 degrees of total hardness).

Plant Aquariums and Paludariums

Number of fish: Figure 4 to 8 quarts (4 to 8 L) of water for each ½ inch (1 cm) of adult fish length (adult fish).

Maintenance of the Dutch aquarium

The care of a plant aquarium is fairly time-consuming; you must spend a few hours a week with it or your handsome underwater garden will soon become an unsightly wilderness. The following things are especially important in the proper care of the plant aquarium:

If you supplement the CO_2 content artificially, the cover must be tightly closed so that the carbon dioxide (CO_2), the most important plant nutrient, does not escape from the water.

The lighting must be sufficiently strong. You are better off choosing the economical fluorescent tubes, which can be hung as close as possible over the aquarium in an unshaded lamp or large light fixture.

Bottom heat (heating cable or heating pad) is recommended because the plants should be situated in well-perfused, warm ground.

The filter is not so important as in a fish aquarium because the few, mostly small fish can hardly pollute the water with their waste products. It is enough if the filter processes one half the aquarium water in one hour. But because the plants do like to stand in flowing water, the filter should be able to raise a gentle current. If supplemental CO_2 is used, the tank should not be aerated with additional diffuser stones.

Water processing may be necessary, either by means of an ion-exchanger (good advice in the pet store) or through peat filtering, because some of the most attractive plants, like the cryptocorynes, *Cabomba, Rotala,* and *Hygrophila,* need soft, slightly acidic water.

Fertilization is one of the most important maintenance factors. When the tank is set up, a slow-release fertilizer should be added to the ground medium. Trace elements are better added daily in small amounts so that the plants always have these important nutrients in the same amounts in the water. A good complete fertilizer for water plants is available in the pet store. Fertilizing with CO_2 may be advisable.

Plant care is somewhat more time-consuming than in the "normal" aquarium. If the plant aquarium is to look well cared for and attractive all the time, you must remove the less attractive-looking plants often or trim those that have become too large. Especially closely pruned stem plants that have been chosen for green in the foreground must sometimes be "mowed" every week or be newly planted with cuttings, so that they don't lose their effect. But many plants will not endure constant pruning, so that sometimes you have to raise them in large quantities. For this you need another — or better, several — tanks in another room. Various kinds of plants can then also be raised emersed, because they are more productive and hardier. The strongest young plants and shoots can then be planted as needed.

The Open Aquarium

If the cover of the aquarium is removed, the plants can grow out of the tank and even bloom. In the open aquarium as in the Dutch aquarium, the plant needs are the most important concern. Such a tank creates a very decorative effect if you have it in the corner of a room or use it as a room divider in conjunction with a larger bank of flowers, containers of houseplants, or hydroponic tanks.

If the aquarium is built into a large window of flowering plants, you have to be careful that the daylight does not pour into the tank from the side. Otherwise algae may develop very quickly, and besides, the light coming from the side disturbs the fish.

The form of the open aquarium

The ideal shape would be a rectangular aquarium 30 x 30 x 18 inches (approximately equivalent to 70 x 70 x 50 cm), with a capacity of 70 gallons (265 L), because this size and shape can be lighted most conveniently by a mercury-vapor or halogen lamp. However, this form — as deep as it is wide — is rarely seen in this country, and one must opt either for shallow tanks, or choose one of the columnar type that is becoming popular. In any event, shallow tanks are more suitable for flourescent lighting. Rectangular tanks are usually placed in a corner of a right-angled seating arrangement. Anyone who has room enough, should certainly not forego the pleasure of a larger tank, for such strong plants like *Nymphaea lotus*, the larger *Echinodorus* species, the blue-flowered and fragrant *Hygrophila corymbosa*, and many others need a container of double the length to be able to develop to their impressive single flowers or groups of them. The largest readily available tanks have a capacity of 100 to 125 gallons (400 – 500 L) and measure 72 x 18 x 18 inches (180 x 45 x 45 cm).

Arranging an open aquarium

In principle, an open aquarium is the same as a planted aquarium, except that the plants that quicky grow out of the water (like hygrophila, echinodorus, lobelia) must be planted in the background and along the sides of the tank so that they won't be disturbed by feeding and cleaning.

Furthermore, when planting, you should be sure to plant those plants that grow out of water especially fast (*Hygrophila* species)

and those that produce especially beautiful flowers *(Lobelia cardinalis)*. At the same time you should not neglect the underwater landscape.

Fish for the open aquarium

You can keep almost all fish that are also suitable for the Dutch aquarium (see page 43). Schools of quiet fish are especially good for open tanks. Unsuitable are the darting and aggressive kinds.

In the open aquarium you should not try to keep the lively zebra fish of the *Danio* and *Brachydanio* genera or the hatchetfish, which, including the span of their pectoral fin, can take up as much as 3 feet (1 m).

Number of fish: Do not overfill the tank with fish. There should not be more than 40 to 60 small fish in a tank that is 48 inches (1.40 m.) long.

Important note: Even if you are only keeping quiet fish, you should glue a glass strip about 4 inches (10 cm) wide around the edge of the container (with silicone glue). It is possible sometimes that even the quiet fish can occasionally try (during pursuit or courtship) to jump out of the tank. Many fish jump directly at the edge or into the corner so in most instances the glass strip will frustrate the attempted escape.

Care of the open aquarium

Lighting must be so arranged that the plants in the upper part of the aquarium have enough room.

Bottom heat can also be used in the open aquarium.

The filter (strength) must be suited to the fish inhabitants; additional aeration with a diffuser stone is not needed.

Fertilization should not be neglected. A soil fertilizer is necessary, with later fertiliza-

Plant Aquariums and Paludariums

tion with a liquid fertilizer and possibly daily with iron and trace elements.

Plant care: Special rules for plant care are not necessary. You can care for the plants in the open aquarium as in any other tank. They only need not be pruned.

Planting suggestions

Back wall: In shady spots *Bolbitis heudelotti* or *Microsorium (Polypodium) pteropus,* in pots in the upper third of the wall cryptocorynes, which in sufficient dampness will bloom above the surface of the water.

Background: A group each of the red and green *Hygrophila corymbosa;* in addition a group each of *Hygrophila difformis, Alternanthera reineckii, Limnophila aquatica;* in addition an *Echinodorus horemanni*, two *Echinodorus bleheri*, and a group of *Cabomba piauhyensis.*

Middle ground: On the side a group each of *Ammannia senegalensis, Cabomba aquatica* (or *Limnophila sessiliflora*). As a focal point, three dark-green *Nymphaea lotus*, together with groups of *Hemianthus micranthemoides* and *Cryptocoryne cordata.*

Foreground: On the sides a group each of *Cryptocoryne balansae* and *Ammannia gracilis;* in the middle a larger group of *Cryptocoryne x willisii* and a small group of *Echinodorus tenellus;* in addition an *Aponogeton ulvaceus* or a group of *Vallisneria asiatica var. biwaensis.*

Ventilation of the living room: Ordinarily the air in our houses is too dry, but over a period of time a considerable amount of water evaporates from an aquarium without a cover that is maintained at 77°F (25°C). The increased humidity can lead to damp wall corners and damage to the rugs. Therefore the rooms in which an open aquarium is located must be well ventilated at all times

Small aquariums with various tropical plants. Background: left, *Echinodorus* and *Vallisneria*, right, *Aponogeton* and *Sagittaria*; center, *Echinodorus* (young plants); foreground: *Echinodorus tenellus* and other small foreground plants.

and be kept at a constant temperature of 70 to 73°F (21 to 23°C). Rooms in which the temperature falls below 64°F (18°C) at night are not suitable for an open aquarium.

The Paludarium

The paludarium has long been known to keepers of terrarium animals. Aquarium fanciers and lovers of aquatic plants have only recently also discovered the beauty of a paludarium.

What is a paludarium?

A paludarium (from Latin *palus* = marsh) is a large glass tank in which a swamp landscape is simulated.

The plants: In the paludarium plants are kept that settle along stream banks in nature. Especially attractive design elements in paludariums are the epiphytes. These are plants that in deep forests perch as "air plants" on trees or on roots of other plants, though they are not parasitic. These plants can be used to decorate back and side walls or you can bind them to epiphyte supports, such as a large tree limb.

Plant Aquariums and Paludariums

The animals: Depending on the size and the arrangement, fish can live in a paludarium, as can amphibians (frogs, salamanders, or toads) or reptiles (turtles, nonpoisonous water snakes, or lizards).

Note: The animals in a paludarium are not decorative features! Whoever intends to keep aquarium fish or terrarium animals in a paludarium should have read the literature on the subject and be fully informed about the needs of these animals.

Arrangement of the paludarium

In the paludariums that are described below you can keep plants alone, but also you can install all the kinds of fish that are suggested for the Dutch aquarium (see page 43).

The size: If you want to keep animals in your paludarium, the life requirements of the inhabitants — the animals as well as the plants — will determine the arrangement. Unless you want to confine yourself to the paludarium-like mini-greenhouse (see page 50 and photograph on page 47), you need a glass tank of at least 47 inches (120 cm) in length, 20 inches (50 cm) in width (the wider the better), and at least 31 inches (80 cm) high (and higher is better).

The tank: Glass tanks of the specified size are seldom available ready-made, most glass tanks are much lower and narrower. You must order them from a glazier or — provided you are handy with tools — make it yourself. Let the staff of the pet store advise you; many pet stores can tell you about the manufacturers who build aquariums to special sizes and also who manufacture suitable paludariums. You can, however, take an ordinary aquarium and mount an addition of suitable height that is closed on top. Both parts are glued together with silicone rubber. If you try this,

be careful that the glue doesn't run down the glass and obscure the viewing surface.

The doors: These are necessary so that you can move things inside the paludarium, take care of the plants, and feed the animals. In low paludariums (about 31 inches [80 cm] high) a trap door in the top (fastened with hinges) will do the job. High paludariums need sliding doors in a side wall or on both side walls. The doors slide up and down on plastic tracks and must close so tightly that no small paludarium inhabitant can ever squeeze through any sort of a crack.

Ventilation: Animals and plants need fresh air. In unventilated tanks the animals will soon become ill and the plants will mildew. The simplest ventilation methods are broad slits in each side wall that are covered with plastic gauze or sievelike perforated plates of PVC. So that the whole tank is evenly perfused by fresh air, the air slits should be as low as possible on one side (depending on the water level and directly under the "roof" on the other side.

Illumination: Daylight is not sufficient. The paludarium needs artificial light (fluorescent bulbs, mercury-vapor, or halogen lamps). The strength of the light depends on the light requirements of the plants and animals.

Heating: A heating pad that lies underneath the paludarium outside is practical. For heating cables and heating rods, holes must be cut in a side wall when the tank is built, in which PVC supports are then glued. The wires for the heating elements will be threaded through these supports and all fastened with silicon rubber.

The filter: The simplest to operate is a thermofilter or a motorized interior filter. The wires to and from an outside filter must be threaded through the PVC supports.

The ground: You can use aquarium stones

Plant Aquariums and Paludariums

with an underlayer of slow-release fertilizer.
The water: It should be filled to a third at most to half the height of the tank. But this is only right for keeping fish and/or plants! If you are keeping terrarium animals, read the literature about them!

Back and side walls: You can decorate the walls like those of an aquarium. A paludarium will look very nice if you add walls of stone or cork bark in which space has been left for compost, or plant holders have been built in.

Planting the paludarium

The charm of paludarium plantings is the decorative combination of water plants and attractive land plant species, for example some of the epiphytic plants.

Water plants: All of the aquarium plants described in this book (see page 56) will thrive sumberged; many of them also live emergent in a paludarium. You can thus plant the water part like an open aquarium (see page 45).

Epiphytic plants: To these belong the bromeliads, the orchids, staghorn ferns, philodendrons, and similar air and climbing plants. They are attached to an epiphyte branch or set in compost or in containers on the back and side walls (above the surface of the water!).

Epiphyte branches: Branches of robinia (*Robinia pseudacacia*), also called acacia, are excellent for this purpose. They can be wrapped in cork bark, to make them larger or to provide better "sitting surfaces" for the plants. It looks especially attractive if a branch has grown so oddly and large that it reaches the whole length of the paludarium. You can also make yourself an epiphyte branch out of round cork bark pieces that you have carefully glued together or screwed together with plastic screws.

Attaching the epiphyte branch: The branch must be attached above the surface of the water, because fresh wood will rot in water, but even more important, the epiphytic plants cannot stand to have "their feet" in water constantly. How you fasten epiphytes to the branch (with silicone rubber, PVC supports, or screws) depends on what material you have used to decorate the back and side walls.

Attaching the plants: The plants, potted or not, can be bound to the bark with the help of strong plant wire or a rugged plastic string. Flowerpots are concealed with cork bark. The root ball of the unpotted plants are wrapped in sphagnum moss, which holds moisture and keeps the root ball from drying out.

Epiphytes for large paludariums over 31 inches (80 cm) long and over 39 inches (1 m) high: Large bromeliads: *Guzmania, Aregelia, Vriesea* species; orchids: *Phalaenopsis, Cattleya, Laelia, Brassavola* species, their various crosses and the cultivated forms of them; ferns: *Asplenium nidusavis*, the bird's-nest fern, and the *Platycerium* species; climbing plants: *Philodendron scandens, Scindapsus aureus, Setcreasia purpurea* and *Gynura aurantiaca;* cactuses: *Zygocactus truncatus* (Christmas cactus), *Rhipsaphyllopsis graeseri* (Easter cactus).

Epiphytes for small paludariums under 30 inches (80 cm) long and 40 inches (1 m) high: Small bromeliads: *Tillandsia* species, *Crypthanthus* species; orchids: *Masdevallia*, small *Epidendrum* and *Cirrhopetalum* species, climbing plants and epiphytic cactuses (as in the large paludarium).

You can keep submersed and emersed *Microsorium (Polypodium) pteropus* and *Bolbitis heudelotii* on the decorated paludarium wall, and climbing plants will also clamber up.

Plant Aquariums and Paludariums

Plant care: You should water the emersed plants regularly with aquarium water; the fertilizer it contains will be sufficient for the easily satisfied epiphytes. You can also spray the plants with water mornings and evenings using a fine flower mister. (The fish are fed the same way as in the aquarium.)

Important: Land plants in pots are fertilized with ordinary fertilizer, aquarium plants with water-plant fertilizer. No flower fertilizer should get into the aquarium, for it contains nitrates that will poison the environment of the water animals.

Mini-greenhouses

The room greenhouses that have recently become available are not proper paludariums, because they are not suitable for keeping animals. They are usually offered completely planted. You can have much pleasure with these little greenhouses if you take care of the plants according to their needs. Unfortunately the contents of such a greenhouse are not always ideal. European sundew *(Drosera)* and the American Venus flytrap *Dionaea muscipula)* — both insectivorous plants from the bogs — thrive without additional heating. But often added to these are other insectivorous plants that grow badly under the given environmental conditions. Then in between the bog plants, which need acid soil, are also houseplants that can't bear acid soil, so the proud display of plants doesn't last long. You should modify the planting if necessary.

Care: Most greenhouses are not tight in the corners and at the roof, so the dampness quickly evaporates. You must therefore seal them with silicone rubber or mist them daily at least once — if needed, more often — with a fine-spray plant mister. Also you should provide sufficient light. Daylight is often not enough. The bog plants, especially, that are planted in most of these little greenhouses are extraordinarily light-hungry. For larger greenhouses, therefore, artificial lighting is necessary.

Note: Anyone who has little space but would like a few pretty water and swamp plants can fill a shallow dish with a pebble-peat mixture and water and arrange some plants decoratively in it (see photograph page 40). You need high humidity and must therefore spray them with water daily.

Plant Damage and Ailments

If you grow your aquarium plants in optimal light and at the correct temperature, provide them with all the nutrients, and do not forget to change a portion of the water regularly, you will have scarcely any problems with plant illnesses or deficiency symptoms. Growth problems and plant injuries are almost always attributable to failures in care.

Damage from Fish and Other Animals

Fish and snails

They cause only minor damage to leaves and stems. Fish eat young shoots and also tips and edges of leaves, especially of finely feathered plants. Snails sometimes scrape little holes in the middle of leaves.
Remedy: Healthy, flourishing plants survive such damage.

Insects

Plant lice (aphids), red spider mites, or whiteflies can colonize emergent plants.
Cause: Usually the air is too dry.
Remedy: The only controls possible are mechanical and biological ones. Insecticides are poisonous to fish!
For a light infestation: Aphids and spider mites can be crushed with the fingers; heavily infested plant parts can be cut away. Or the plant lice can be fed to the fish — live-bearing and egg-laying killifish love to eat these parasites: push the infested stems under the water, turn floating leaves over and plunge them a few times, and the aphids will rinse off.
For heavy infestations: It may be possible to introduce natural predators of the damaging insect. This is only possible in a closed tank! For instance, aphids are eaten by ladybugs and red spider mites by predatory mites. Parasitic fungi for insect control are sometimes available. Get advice in the pet store.

Injuries from Improper Maintenance

Insufficient light

Symptoms: Plants thin and weak. Leaves pale green to yellowish, stems thin. With rosette plants small leaves on a weak stalk. Stem plants thinly leaved, leggy, grow strongly toward light source and stunted, lower stem part sometimes completely leafless. Algae appear on pebbles.
Causes: Use of too few or too weak lamps, of lamps without reflectors or over-age fluorescent tubes. Too short a span of lighting (less than 12 hours a day). Algae or chalk deposit on the roof glass. Too thick a cover of floating plants.
Remedy: Proper lighting (see page 15).

Wrong light color

Symptoms and cause: High, leggy plants with fluorescent lamps with a very strong red portion of the spectrum. Low, stunted growth with a very high blue portion. Stunted growth and same symptoms as for poor light with green and yellow light.
Remedy: Proper lighting (see page 15).

Incorrect water temperature

Symptoms: At too high a temperature, extra-long internodes and small leaves on stem plants, weak growth in rosette plants (symptoms similar to light deficiency). In water that is too cold plants stop their growth and die after a time.
Cause: Too high or too low a temperature or else incorrect proportion of warmth and light intensity or of warmth and nutrients. The higher the temperature, the faster the plant grows. If light or nourishment is not sufficient, there will be growth disturbances.
Remedy: Examine temperature, light, and nutrient supply and correct the error.

Plant Damage and Ailments

Anoxic soil
Symptoms: Ascent of gas bubbles as soon as you poke the bottom with a small stick, stunted plant growth, snails no longer dig in by day, roots of the plants weak, begin to rot, finally blacken.
Causes: Ground compacted or too old.
Remedy: Bore into the ground with your fingers, siphon out the mulm at those places. This procedure, as well as firmly pressing on the floor surface, will allow the gases produced by decay to escape. Two days later clean the filter, a week later fertilize the plants. If the plants do not recover in two weeks at the latest, renew the floor material.
Prevention measure: Don't leave the floor material in the aquarium for longer than three years.

Nutritional Disturbances
Oxygen deficiency
Symptoms: Fish become ill. With a long-term oxygen deficiency the plants suffer. Abundant algae growth.
Causes: Insufficient light or nutrient deficiencies so that the plants cannot perform photosynthesis, thus producing no oxygen; or the nitrogen breakdown in the aquarium no longer functions, because the bacteria in the filter work too slowly or not at all. Consequence: Water is overburdened with waste products and excess carbon dioxide.
Remedy: Check the light, filter, fish, and all other maintenance procedures.

Carbon dioxide (CO_2) deficiency
Symptoms: The plants remain much smaller and grow more slowly than plants that have been fertilized with CO_2. Rough deposits on the leaves (biogenic decalcification).
Causes: CO_2 deficiency can even arise with optimal maintenance and nourishment because of strongly agitated water or aeration with a stone diffuser, thus allowing the CO_2 to escape into the air.
Remedy: Fertilize with CO_2.

Carbon dioxide (CO_2) excess
Symptoms: Fish gasp at the water surface (danger of suffocation, as in nitrite poisoning).
Cause: Oxygen deficiency arising from faults in maintenance, overfertilization with CO_2, most often a dirty filter, but also bad lighting, too many fish, keeping of plants and animals with different life requirements.
Remedy: Check over the care procedures. Measure the addition of CO_2 better, turn off the equipment at night, or hook up to a light-timer switch. In community aquariums, improve the basic care conditions!

Leaves of ailing plants (from left to right): heavy damage from excess nitrate; leaves decaying and perforated from cryptocoryne rot; light leaf veins, yellowy, glassy leaf tissue caused by chlorosis; green leaf veins and yellow leaf tissue caused by manganese deficiency.

Potassium deficiency
Symptoms: Yellowing of the margins of young leaves, chlorosis (see page 53).

Cause: Potassium is removed from the water supply at the waterworks, thus inducing a potassium deficiency.
Remedy: Regular fertilization.

Phosphate excess
Symptoms: Buildup of iron phosphate causes brown or black coloring and death of the leaves. Iron deficiency. If there is also excess of nitrate, then the explosive increase of algae.
Cause: Partial water exchange neglected.
Remedy: Carry out partial water exchange regularly without fail (the excess of phosphates will thus be removed).

Nitrate excess
One of the most dangerous plant diseases, cryptocoryne disease or rot, is probably induced by overfertilization with nitrogen compounds, especially nitrates. Imported plants are more at risk than those raised by local dealers; the most resistant seem to be bright-green, small-leaved species.
Symptoms: In the beginning small holes in the leaves or along the margins (they look as if they'd been eaten by fish or snails), but then within a few days the whole plant is attacked or the whole stand of cryptocorynes even may collapse and rot.
Causes: In contrast to many other kinds of plants, which live in nitrate-rich water, cryptocorynes are evidently not able to split nitrates and extract their nutrients, especially ammonium. They probably take the nitrate and store it in their body cells, along with other materials not being used at the moment. There are different theories about the cause of the disease.

One theory is that the plants react to the sudden changes in the aquarium environment as if to a shock. (Changes like water change after a long time, fertilization after a long period of hunger, change of a long-exhausted fluorescent tube, or cleaning of a very dirty filter.) To overcome the shock, the plants must use their stored reserves. Thus the stored nitrates are also free again and create poisonous nitrogen compounds in the plants that cause them to die.

Another theory proposes that the plants are not shocked but that the sudden improvement of the aquarium milieu stimulates their life processes and with it the capacity for photosynthesis. Because the plants are now producing more oxygen, however, which is also dispersed throughout their own bodies, the various chemical compounds in the plant body are oxidized and precipitate, that is, they become unavailable. These precipitated materials then clog the plant's interior circulation system so that it dies.

Both theories emphasize that the main reason for cryptocoryne rot is evidently bad nourishment, and the triggering factor a major change in the aquarium.
Remedy: Improve the aquarium milieu immediately. Suck out dead plant material. Leave the plants alone. They will usually be restored in a few weeks.
Preventive measure: To avoid shocks, try to maintain a stable aquarium milieu.

Deficiency of trace elements
A deficiency of iron, the most important trace element, will produce chlorosis.
Symptoms: Yellow leaves that become brittle and glassy and finally die.
Causes: Too little fertilizer, potassium deficiency, overfertilization with phosphates. In a well-fertilized aquarium also too high a carbonate or total hardness and pH over 7.
Remedy: Regular fertilizing with a complete, iron-rich water-plant fertilizer or daily addition of trace elements (see page 14).

Plant Damage and Ailments

Manganese deficiency
Symptoms: Yellow leaves but the veins remain green.
Cause: Incomplete iron fertilizer.
Remedy: Fertilizing with a complete fertilizer. Do not just use iron fertilizer.

Leaf Injury from Chemicals

Symptoms: Algae control substances, fish medicines, and snail poisons can produce leaf damage of different kinds. The individual plant species react with varying degrees of sensitivity and most of them not right away. But a few weeks after the use of one of these substances the leaves may become yellow or brown.
Remedy: After using any chemical control substances, change the water; more than half of the water can be changed.
Note: Follow exactly the manufacturer's instructions for the use of chemical substances!

Control of Algae

The development of algae cannot be prevented. At the least you introduce them to the tank with newly bought plants or with water fleas from the garden pond. Newly established aquariums, particularly, are often afflicted by a plague of algae. But the various different kinds of algae can also appear in the older aquarium. Therefore you need to take care that they don't get the upper hand or else try to keep them from appearing in the first place.

Blue-green algae
Symptoms: Thick, slippery, blue-green, violet, or brown-black coating on the floor, stones, and plants. Strong-, boggy-smelling water.

Causes: In newly established aquariums, the not-yet-stable aquarium milieu. In older aquariums, compacted floor, too much fish food, overfertilization, death and decay of tubifex in the ground, badly maintained filter, water supply containing nitrates, changing water too seldom, constant oxygen deficiency.
Remedy: In newly established aquariums remove the coating by hand or very carefully suck it up with the hose, at best several times daily. In older aquariums, clean the filter and change part of the water and suck up the mulm. Two days later fertilize the plants (iron) to strengthen them; for fast water improvement, plant *Sagittaria,* waterweed, *Aponogeton,* and *Hygrophila,* all of which take up nitrogenous waste products. As algae eaters, the simplest: red ramshorn snails. Temperature not above 77°F (25°C)!

Gravel algae (bottom-living diatons)
Symptoms: Thin, brown, somewhat rough deposits on aquarium walls, decorations, and plants.
Causes: Light deficiency, oxygen deficiency, too high a nitrate content.
Remedy: Increase the light intensity or extend the length of the lighting day. Possibly install snails and algae-eating fish.

Red algae
Symptoms: Smutty green to black spots on plants, wood, and stones (black dot algae), filaments (beard algae), or small clusters (black brush algae).
Causes: Introduced on plants imported from Southeast Asia (especially cryptocorynes), nitrate-rich, hard water with a pH over 7 (CO_2 deficiency!). Usually only unhealthy plants will be attacked.
Remedy: Red algae are very tenacious; therefore cut off the leaves, since you can

neither suction them off or remove them by hand without damaging the leaves. Fertilization with iron or with CO_2 will usually make them disappear. The water may also be filtered through peat (for at least as long as two months) in order to lower water hardness and pH. Change over-age fluorescent light tubes. Install algae eaters.

Green algae
Symptoms: Differs according to type of green algae. On decorations, plants, and aquarium floor, wool-like coating (fur algae), dark-green spots (green dot algae), branching filaments (green cluster algae), long filaments that enwrap the plants (green thread algae), unattached tangles (tangle algae). The microscopic little green floating algae of the genus *Volvox* turn the water into an opaque green broth.

Causes: Excess phosphate and high nitrate values. *Volvox* is sometimes introduced with water fleas, but it also arises in brightly lighted tanks with superfluous food and overfertilization.

Remedy: For *Volvox,* complete darkening of the aquarium for three to four days, installation of an oxygenator (enrich the water with oxygen). Best, use UV light, if you can arrange to do so, for as long as it takes for the floating algae to disappear. With a diatom filter (pet store) the *Volvox* can simply be filtered out. Green thread algae can be removed carefully by hand. To deprive the green algae of the conditions they need to live, lower the high phosphate and nitrogen content for certain by means of regular water changes. Perhaps install algae-eating fish.

Aquarium Plants

Anubias barteri
Family Araceae (Arum family)

Aponogeton crispus
Family Aponogetonaceae
(Aponogeton family)

Aponogeton rigidifolius
Family Aponogetonaceae
(Aponogeton family)

Distribution: Tropical West Africa
Appearance: Up to 15½ inches
(40 cm) tall. Rosette plant with
thick, creeping rhizomes. Stemmed
leaves, firm, leathery. Quick-grow-
ing in paludarium, blooms repeatedly. Grows more slowly in
aquarium.
Varieties: *Anubias barteri var. barteri* — about 10 inches (25 cm)
high, leaves oval-lanceolate; *Anubias barteri var. glabra* — about
16½ inches (40 cm) high, leaves
lanceolate; *Anubias barteri var.
nana* (see drawing) — about 4
inches (10 cm) high, leaves variable, mostly ovate with acute tips.
Care: Protect rhizomes and roots
when planting! Ground fertilization
necessary, warmed ground and
CO_2-fertilization recommended.
Light: 30 watts per 25 gallons (100 L).
Water: 72°-82°F (22-28°C);
2-15 degrees carbonate hardness;
pH 6.0-7.5.
Propagation: Side sprouts from
rhizome; rhizome division.
Placement: Tall-growing varieties
singly or in groups in center and
background, smaller ones in groups
in foreground.

Distribution: Sri Lanka.
Appearance: Up to 20 inches
(50 cm) high. Rosette plant with
tubers as food storage areas.
Stemmed leaves, lanceolate to long-
elliptical; leaf margin extremely
wavy. Blooms whitish, single
spike, bisexual, self-fertile; throws
a blooming stem above the water
surface. Different appearance in
different areas of the world. With
crosses and similar varieties sometimes forms the "Crispus group."
(Photograph page 10).
Care: Only submersed culture is
possible. Nutrient-rich earth and
iron fertilizer. Observe resting
period.
Light: 50 watts and more per 26½
gallons (100 L).
Water: 72-86°F (22-30°C);
2-15 degrees carbonate hardness;
pH 6.0-7.5.
Propagation: Seeds, artificial pollination required.
Placement: Singly in center, in
large aquariums also in groups.

Distribution: Sri Lanka.
Appearance: Over 24 inches
(60 cm) high. Rosette plants with
rhizomes (not tubers!). Leaves
stemmed, stiffly upright, somewhat
brittle, rough and hard, dark-green
to olive brown, lightly wavy along
the edge. Flower single spike,
greenish, self-fertile. (Photograph
page 19).
Care: No resting period, since
there are no tubers for food storage.
Very sensitive. Important are clean
water and unfertilized ground; fertilization with fertilizers containing
iron. With CO_2 fertilization will
tolerate somewhat harder water.
Transplants poorly. When maintenance is not good, leaves will
become spotty and curl under.
Light: 50 watts per 26½ gallons
(100 L).
Water: 72-82°F (22-28°C);
1-3 degrees carbonate hardness;
pH 5.5-6.5.
Propagation: Side sprouts on rhizome. Extremely difficult to raise
from seed.
Placement: Singly in large
aquariums.

Rosette Plants

Aponogeton ulvaceus
Family Aponogetonaceae
(Aponogeton family)

Distribution: Madagascar
Appearance: Up to 24 inches
(60 cm) high. Rosette plant with
round, smooth tuber. Leaves
stemmed, markedly wavy and often
turned on themselves, bright green,
almost transparent, reddish in very
bright light. Flowers double spiked,
yellow, self-fertile.
Care: Ground fertilization not
absolutely necessary, but liquid fertilizer with iron should be applied.
Grows well in moving water. In
poor light grows very tall and thin.
Observe resting period.
Light: 50 watts per 25 gallons
(100 L).
Water: 64-82°F (18-28°C);
2-15 degrees carbonate hardness;
pH 5.5-7.5.
Propagation: Seeds.
Placement: Singly.

Aponogeton undulatus
Family Aponogetonaceae (Aponogeton family)

Distribution: India and northern
Indo-China.
Appearance: About 16 inches (40
cm) tall. Rosette plants with tubers.
Leaves stemmed, bright green; leaf
margins wavy, especially strongly
in a bright spot; in weak light the
leaves are almost smooth. Produces
flowers very seldom; an adventitious plant almost always develops
on the flower stem (photograph
page 19).
Care: Iron fertilizer and ground
somewhat rich in nutrients recommended. Observe resting period!
Light: 50 watts per 25 gallons
(100 L).
Water: 72-82°F (22-28°C); 5-12
degrees carbonate hardness;
pH 6.5-7.5.
Propagation: Adventitious plants.
As soon as the adventitious plants
have a small tuber, roots, and about
five to six leaves, you can cut it off
and plant it or bend the stem down
and fasten it.
Placement: Singly; also in groups
in very large aquariums.

Barclaya longifolia
Family Numphaeceae (Water lily
family)

Distribution: Burma, Andaman
Islands, southern Thailand, Vietnam
Appearance: 10-20 inches (25-50
cm) tall. Rosette plant with small
rhizomes. Leaves stemmed, lanceolate; leaf margins wavy, more so in
strong light. Blooms repeatedly in
the aquarium (emergent or submerged). Submerged flowers
remain closed but produce seeds
that will germinate like the emergent ones. Olive-green and red-
brown to deep-red forms available
commercially. (Photograph inside
front cover).
Care: Iron-rich fertilizer not absolutely essential, ground fertilizer
and CO_2 fertilization recommended. Endures transplanting
badly; for several weeks afterward
monitor rhizome for rotten spots.
Red plants need more light than
olive-green ones.
Light: About 50 watts per 25 gallons (100 L).
Water: 72-82°F (22-28°C); 2-12
degrees carbonate hardness;
pH 6.0-7.0.
Propagation: Seeds or side growth
from rhizome.
Placement: Singly.

Rosette Plants

Crinum natans
Family Amaryllidaceae (Amaryllis family)

Distribution: Africa.
Appearance: 20-30 inches (50-75 cm) tall. Bulb plants. Leaves arise from the ground without stems, luminous green, burled; in good light the leaves are more strongly burled than in shadow. Blooms white, seldom blooms in aquarium; blooms rise some 30 inches (75 cm), towering over the surface of the water.
Care: Bright light. Ground rich in nutrients; in hard water poor growth. Cannot tolerate trypaflavin (contained in some fish medications and algae control products).
Light: 50 watts per 25 gallons (100 L).
Water: 75-86°F (24-30°C); 2-10 degrees carbonate hardness; pH 5.5-7.0.
Propagation: Rhizome runners, bulblets.
Placement: Singly; background in large, high aquariums.
Tip: All *Crinum* species are also recommended as swamp plants for large paludariums, enclosed flower windows, or for small greenhouses.

Cryptocoryne affinis (C. haerteliana)
Prolific Cryptocoryne
Family Araceae (Arum family)

Distribution: Malayan peninsula.
Appearance: 4-12 inches (10-30 cm) high. Rosette plant with small rhizome. Leaves stemmed; submersed leaves long ovate to lanceolate, somewhat burled and wavy; upper leaf surface dark green, underside wine red. Under emergent culture shorter and smoother leaves, often blooming as well, the standard violet-black, the throat whitish-green. Also blooms in the aquarium sometimes. (Photographs pages 5 and 39.)
Care: Undemanding; tolerates lowered light. With regular fertilizing (iron) large plant groups will develop. Susceptible to cryptocoryne rot after changes of any kind.
Light: 30 watts per 25 gallons (100 L).
Water: 72-82°F (22-28°C); 3-15 degrees carbonate hardness; pH 6.0-7.
Propagation: Runners.
Placement: In groups, according to the aquarium size in the foreground or the middle ground.

Cryptocoryne cordata
Water trumpet
Family Araceae (Arum family)

Distribution: Malayan peninsula.
Appearance: Up to 20 inches (50 cm) high. A principal representative of the *Cryptocoryne cordata* group. Each is very different in appearance depending on its environmental needs. Described by many different names (for example, *Cryptocoryne blassii, cryptocoryne kerii*). Leaves long-stemmed, ovate to cordate, upper side green mottled with violet, or reddish brown; underside cream-colored, red-brown to violet. In emergent culture, flowers, standards yellow to red-brown, throat yellow. (Photograph page 10).
Care: Very demanding. Forms with oval leaves are easier to grow than those with cordate leaves. Nutrient-rich, warmed ground, regular iron fertilization. Do not injure roots!
Light: 50 watts per 25 gallons (100 L).
Water: 75-82°F (24-28°C); 2-8 degrees carbonate hardness; pH 5.5-7.0.
Propagation: Runners.
Placement: Singly or in groups.

Rosette Plants

Cryptocoryne pontederiifolia
Family Araceae (Arum family)

Cryptocoryne wendtii
Family Araceae (Arum family)

Cryptocoryne x willisii
Family Araceae (Arum family)

Distribution: Sumatra, Borneo.
Appearance: About 14 inches
(35 cm) high. Rosette plant with
thin rhizomes. Leaves stemmed,
oval lanceolate, somewhat burled,
green, undersides pale rose color.
Stem long, brownish. In emergent
culture grows more compact and
sturdier, then also blooms regularly.
Care: Nutrient-rich ground, iron
fertilizer. Transplant as seldom as
possible, otherwise growth is
stunted. Roots are sensitive.
Light: About 50 watts per 25
gallons (100 L).
Water: 72-82°F (22-28°C);
2-12 degrees carbonate hardness;
pH 6.0-7.2.
Propagation: Runners
Placement: Singly in bright light,
then grows compact and broad. In
shadow (for instance in background
of tank) grows taller and narrower,
therefore should be in groups there.
Tip: Stable plants, so good for
robust fish.

Distribution: Sri Lanka.
Appearance: 4-16 inches (10-40
cm) high. Many varieties and commercial forms with green, olive-
green or red-brown leaves, which
vary in size, form, and color.
Appearance is also dependent on
light; in light that is too weak red-
brown plants grow green, grow
taller and thinner, and wavy leaf
margins become smooth. Blooms
in emergent culture. (Photograph
page 19).
Care: Fertilized ground, iron fertilizer. Thin stands regularly. Subject
to cryptocoryne rot with quick
changes of culture conditions.
Light: About 50 watts per 25 gallons (100 L).
Water: 75-82°F (24-28°C);
2-15 degrees carbonate hardness;
pH 6.5-7.5.
Propagation: Runners.
Placement: Singly, groups (in
dense groups all varieties grow
taller and thinner); small varieties
in foreground, the larger ones in the
middle ground.

Distribution: Sri Lanka.
Appearance: Up to 6 inches (15
cm) high. Leaves stemmed, long
oval to lanceolate, green; stems
brown to green. Produces abundant
runners. Grows more compactly in
emergent culture, when it may
bloom. Standards violet, throats
yellowish to violet. (Photograph
page 19.)
Care: Fertilized ground, frequent
water changes with regular fertilization afterward. Thin the stands
from time to time and protect
against algae.
Light: 50 watts per 25 gallons
(100 L).
Water: 72-86°F (22-30°C);
2-15 degrees carbonate hardness;
pH 6.5-7.5.
Propagation: Runners.
Placement: Foreground, set in
groups. The brighter the light, the
shallower and broader the plants
will be (ground cover).

Rosette Plants

Echinodorus amazonicus
Slender-leaved Amazon
Family Alismataceae (Water plantain family)

Distribution: Brazil.
Appearance: Up to 20 inches (50 cm) high. Rosette plant with short rhizomes. Leaves lanceolate, small, often slightly curved (ensiform), green; stems rather short.
Care: Tolerates soft water better than hard; with high degrees of carbonate hardness grows poorly despite good fertilization, then CO_2-fertilization necessary. Light soil and iron fertilization are important.
Light: 50 watts per 25 gallons (100 L).
Water: 72-82°F (22-28°C); 2-12 degrees carbonate hardness; pH 6.5-7.2.
Propagation: Adventitious plants on submerged flower stem.
Placement: Singly, in large aquariums also in groups.
Note: *Echinodorus* tends to be called swordplant or Amazon swordplant regardless of species; ordering by scientific name is especially advisable.

Echinodorus bleheri
Family Alismataceae (Water plantain family)

Distribution: Tropical South America.
Appearance: Over 20 inches (50 cm) high. Leaves stemmed, lanceolate, dark-green. The plants resemble *Echinodorus amazonicus*, although with broader leaves, and *Echinodorus maior*.
Care: Can stand higher carbonate hardness but needs regular iron fertilization or the center leaves become yellow and glassy.
Light: 50 watts per 25 gallons (100 L) but can also stand less.
Water: 72-86°F (22-30°C); 2-18 degrees carbonate hardness; pH 6.5-7.5.
Propagation: Adventitious plants on flower stem.
Placement: Singly; in larger tanks as group plants in the background.

Echinodorus cordifolius
Swordplant, Elephant ear
Family Alismataceae (Water plantain family)

Distribution: Central and southern North America, Mexico.
Appearance: Over 20 inches (50 cm) high. Stemmed leaves, heart-shaped, shimmering green. Floating leaves long-stemmed. Blooms (white) in open aquarium. (Photographs page 9, 47, and back cover.)
Care: Remove floating leaves; otherwise the plants will shed submersed leaves and will take too much light from the other plants. Heavy fertilization produces abundant growth. In small room aquariums, plant in small pots or prune the roots all around it periodically. Can also be cut back.
Light: 50 watts per 25 gallons (100 L).
Water: 72-82°F (22-28°C); 5-15 degrees carbonate hardness; pH 6.5-7.5.
Propagation: Adventitious plants on a flower stem; sometimes also seeds.
Placement: Singly in aquariums of 55 gallons (200 L) or more; grown best in large open aquariums.

Rosette Plants

Echinodorus horemanii
Family Alismataceae (Water plantain family)

Echinodorus osiris
Family Alismataceae (Water plantain family)

Echinodorus parviflorus
Black Amazon
Family Alismataceae (Water plantain family)

Distribution: Southern Brazil.
Appearance: over 24 inches (60 cm) tall. Short-stemmed leaves, lanceolate, stiff, parchmentlike, dark green, slightly waved along the edge. A red-leaved variety is availble commercially occasionally. (Photograph front cover.)
Care: Prefers cool water to warm. Nutrient-rich ground and regular fertilization (iron) required; CO_2-fertilization recommended.
Light: 50 watts per 25 gallons (100 L).
Water: 64-79°F (18-26°C); 2-15 degrees carbonate hardness; pH 6.5-7.5.
Propagation: Side sprouts from the rhizome, adventitious plants on the submerged flower stem.
Placement: Singly.

Distribution: Southern Brazil.
Appearance: About 20 inches (50 cm) high. Leaves stemmed, lanceolate, slightly wavy along the edge, green; young leaves (and thus also young plants) reddish. Does not bloom in the aquarium but puts out adventitious plants on the flower stem. (Photograph page 19.)
Care: Tolerates hard water; will grow in weak light. In stronger light, nutrient-rich and regular fertilization (iron) is absolutely necessary, otherwise the plants will starve; the water should then not be colder than 75°F (24°C).
Light: About 50 watts per 25 gallons (100 L).
Water: 64-82°F (18-28°C); 5-18 degrees carbonate hardness; pH 6.5-7.5.
Propagation: Side shoots on the rhizome, adventitious plants on the flower stem.
Placement: Singly.

Distribution: Peru, Bolivia.
Appearance: About 12 inches (30 cm) high. Fast-growing rosette plant with strong rhizomes; with good care grows to a fine specimen with far more than 60 leaves on it. Leaves stemmed, lanceolate, shimmering green; leaf veins often reddish black.
Care: Nutrient-rich ground, regular fertilizing (iron) after each water change.
Light: 50 watts per 25 gallons (100 L).
Water: 68-82°F (20-28°C); 2-15 degrees carbonate hardness; pH 6.0-7.8.
Propagation: Adventitious plants on the flower stem.
Placement: Singly in small aquariums; in large tanks in groups (not set too close together), for example to cover the bare stems of background plants.

Rosette Plants

Echinodorus quadricostatus var. xinguensis
Little Amazon
Family Alismataceae (Water plantain family)

Distribution: Rio Xingú, Pará, Brazil.
Appearance: Up to 6 inches (15 cm) high. Leaves stemmed, linear, bright green. Puts out runners prolifically. Grasslike.
Care: Ground fertilization usually not necessary, but iron fertilizing after every water change is required. The brighter the light, the more nutrients will be needed. Thin out groups as soon as it becomes necessary; otherwise algae will develop.
Light: 75 watts per 25 gallons (100 L).
Water: 72-82°F (22-28°C); 2-12 degrees carbonate hardness; pH 6.5-7.5.
Propagation: Runners.
Placement: Foreground (ground-covering plants).

Echinodorus tenellus
Microsagittaria; Pygmy chain
Family Alismataceae (Water plantain family)

Distribution: Brazil to U.S.A.
Appearance: Up to 4 inches (10 cm) high. Rosettes of grassy, unstemmed little leaves, broader in emersed culture. Grasslike.
Varieties: *Echinodorus tenellus var. tenellus* — leaves very small, dark-green to reddish; *Echinodorus tenellus var. parvulus* — leaves somewhat broader, grass green.
Care: Light-requiring, in hard water better to fertilize with CO_2. Allow enough space around single plants because they produce shoots quickly and prolifically. Regular fertilization (iron); thin out overgrown clumps more frquently; if necessary, replace them.
Light: 75 watts and more per 25 gallons (100 L).
Water: 72-86°F (22-30°C); 2-12 degrees carbonate hardness; pH 6.5-7.2.
Propagation: Runners.
Placement: Foreground (grasslike plants).

Nymphaea lotus
Lotus lily, Egyptian water lily, lotus, Egyptian lily, white lily.
Family Nymphaeaceae (Water lilies)

Distribution: East Africa, Madagascar, Southeast Asia.
Appearance: 10-20 inches (25-50 cm) high. Submersed leaves stemmed, roundish to oval, slightly wavy with deeply indented base. Floating leaves very long stemmed, more or less heart-shaped with large serrated edges. Blooms yellow-white, fragrant, up to 4 inches (10 cm) in diameter; night-blooming, self-fertile. (Photograph page 20.)
Varieties: *Nymphaea lotus var. viridis* — leaves green, flecked with dark red; *Nymphaea lotus var. rubra* — leaves red with dark-red flecks. Many gradations of color.
Care: If the plants are to bloom, three to five floating leaves must be retained; otherwise cut them off. Compact growth with good light.
Light: 50 watts per 25 gallons (100 L).
Water: 72-82°F (22-28°C); 2-12 degrees carbonate hardness; pH 5.5-7.5.
Propagation: Seeds, runners from rhizomes.
Placement: Singly in large aquariums.

Rosette Plants

Nymphoides aquatica
Banana plant, floating heart.
Family Gentianaceae/Menyanthaceae (Gentian family including the Menyanthaceae)

Distribution: Eastern and southeastern U.S.A. (Florida).
Appearance: About 6 inches (15 cm) high. Submersed leaves long-stemmed, cordate, slightly wavy, bright-green to reddish. At the bottom of the stem axis are banana-shaped roots for nutrient storage; floating leaves coarse, olive-green, underside reddish. After floating leaves flower production, white flowers. After blooming it produces adventitious plants that lack "bananas."
Care: Plant banana roots up to ¼ of their length in the ground or even just press them in and anchor them slightly until they root themselves.
Light: 50 watts or more per 25 gallons (100 L).
Water: 68-82°F (20-28°C); 5-10 degrees carbonate hardness; pH 6.5-7.2.
Propagation: Press adventitious plants or completely formed leaves firmly into damp ground; with sufficient humidity they will root themselves.
Placement: Singly in foreground.

Sagittaria subulata
Arrowhead, Needle sagittaria
Family Alismataceae (Water plantain family)

Distribution: American East Coast, naturalized here and there in South America.
Appearance: Up to 24 inches (60 cm) high. Submersed leaves unstemmed, ribbonlike, blunt. Flowers white, floating on thin stems, raised above the water surface. Fast-growing, produces thick clumps. (Photograph page 26.)
Varieties: Leaf breadth varies. *Sagittaria subulata var. subulata* (see drawing) — up to 12 inches (30 cm) high; *Sagittaria subulata var. gracillima* — 23 to 35 inches (60 to 90 cm) high; *Sagittaria subulata var. kurtziana* — up to 20 inches (50 cm) high. Differentiation is not definite. The larger are described as *forma natans*, the smaller as *forma pusilla*.
Care: Completely undemanding; rejuvenate plantings periodically.
Light: 50 watts or less per 25 gallons (100 L).
Water: 68-82°F (20-28°C); 2-15 degrees carbonate hardness; pH 6.0-7.8.
Propagation: Runners.
Placement: Background.

Samolus parviflorus
Underwater rose
Family Primulaceae (Primrose family)

Distribution: North and South America, West Indies.
Appearance: 4 inches (10 cm) high. Small rosettes up to 3 inches (8 cm) long, short-stemmed, spatulate, bright-green leaves, leaf veins almost white. Resembles rampion. Actually a marsh plant, blooms (white) and fruits with emersed culture. (Photograph page 19.)
Care: Fertilize well; needs much light. Don't plant too deep.
Light: 75 watts per 25 gallons (100 L).
Water: 64-75°F (18-24°C); 5-12 degrees carbonate hardness; pH 6.5-7.5.
Propagation: Not possible in the aquarium.
Placement: Foreground, planted in groups.

Vallisneria asiatica var. biwaensis
Family Hydrocharitaceae (Frog's-bit family)

Distribution: Lake Biwa, Yodo River, Japan.
Appearance: Up to 16 inches (40 cm) high. Submersed rosette plants with short rhizomes. Leaves unstemmed, ribbonlike, spiraled, shimmering green. Blooms on long stems over the surface of the water (Photograph page 10).
Care: Requires light; in weak light the leaves will become smoother. Grows better in tanks without floating plants. Iron fertilizer recommended; otherwise trouble-free.
Light: 75 watts per 25 gallons (100 L).
Water: 68-86°F (20-30°C); 5-15 degrees carbonate hardness; pH 6.0-7.2.
Propagation: Runners.
Placement: Single groups as an eyecatcher; also suitable for side and background plantings.
Note: *Vallisneria* is a variable genus. It is sometimes sold as tape grass or wild celery. Consult wholesaler's lists for availability.

Vallisneria gigantea
Family Hydrocharitaceae (Frog's-bit family)

Distribution: Southeast Asian islands, New Guinea, Philippines.
Appearance: In aquariums over 40 inches (100 cm), in nature up to 80 inches (2 m) high. Leaves unstemmed, ribbonlike, shimmering green. (Photograph page 26).
Care: Only suitable for high aquariums; leaves spread out on water surface and shade other plants. Don't plant too many or too close together. Fertilized ground and additional fertilization with iron fertilizers will produce beautiful large specimens; in thin soil they remain pale and weak. Iron deficiency leads to chlorosis.
Light: 50 watts or more per 25 gallons (100 L).
Water: 64-82°F (18-28°C); 5-15 degrees carbonate hardness; pH 6.0-7.2.
Propagation: Runners.
Placement: Background in high aquariums.

Vallisneria spiralis
Corkscrew vallisneria (*Tortifolia* variety)
Family Hydrocharitaceae (Frog's-bit family)

Distribution: Originally North Africa and southern Europe, today naturalized in the tropics and subtropics of the whole world.
Appearance: Over 20 inches (50 cm). Leaves unstemmed, ribbonlike, blunt. Whitish blooms on spiral stems lie at water surface. (Photographs pages 26 and 29).
Care: Undemanding. One of the oldest aquarium plants. Produces runners prolifically, thus quickly grows to thick stands.
Light: 50 watts per 25 gallons (100 L).
Water: 59°-86°F (15-30°C); 5-12 degrees carbonate hardness; pH 6.5-7.5.
Propagation: Runners.
Placement: Background and sides of large aquariums or in groups in the middle areas or in front corners.

Stem Plants

Alternanthera reineckii
Copperleaf
Family Amaranthaceae (Amaranth family)

Ammannia gracilis
Family Lythraceae (Loosestrife family)

Ammannia senegalensis
Family Lythraceae (Loosestrife family)

Distribution: Tropical America.
Appearance: About 20 inches (50 cm) high. Leaves stemmed, decussate, lanceolate, upper sides olive green to olive brown or red, undersides red-violet. In emersed culture, small white flowers arising at the leaf axil. (Photograph page 20.) Various species and many forms available commercially; best suited for the aquarium is *Alteranthera reineckii*, "small-leaved type."
Care: Iron fertilizer necessary, nutrient-rich planting medium and CO_2-fertilization recommended. With light and nutrient deficiency the red coloration of the leaves fades and their margins become smooth.
Light: 75 watts per 25 gallons (100 L).
Water: 72-86°F (22-30°C); 2-12 degrees carbonate hardness; pH 5.5-7.5.
Propagation: Cuttings; seeds with emersed culture.
Placement: In groups in the foreground or middle ground. Goes well with finely feathered bright-green plants.

Distribution: Tropical Africa.
Appearance: About 20 inches (50 cm) high. Leaves sessile, decussate, linear, olive green to reddish-brown. Blooms small, grouped at leaf axil.
Care: Needs high light, pale, stunted growth in light and nutrient deficiency; iron fertilizer needed to maintain leaf color. If bottoms of stems are bare, plant lower plants in front of them.
Light: 75 watts per 25 gallons (100 L).
Water: 68-82°F (20-28°C); 2-12 degrees carbonate hardness; pH 5.5-7.5.
Propagation: Cuttings; seeds in emergent culture.
Placement: In groups in middle and background or at the sides. Goes well with green plants.
Tip: Also good for paludariums.

Distribution: East and South Africa.
Appearance: About 20 inches (50 cm) high. Leaves sessile, decussate, linear, bright olive brown, leaf margins and tips usually curved under. On emersed stems small, pale lavender blooms in clusters at the leaf axis. (Photograph page 10).
Care: Needs light; iron fertilizer inhibits fading of the color.
Light: 75 watts per 25 gallons (100 L).
Water: 75-86°F (24-30°C); 2 8 degrees carbonate hardness; pH 6.5-7.5.
Propagation: Cuttings; seeds in emergent culture.
Placement: In groups in middle and background as well as at the sides. Works well (as accent) with green plants.

Stem Plants

Bacopa caroliniana
Water hyssop
Family Scrophulariaceae (Figwort family)

Cabomba aquatica
Fanwort
Family Nymphaeaceae (Water lilies)

Cabomba caroliniana
Fanwort, Washington grass, fish grass
Family Nymphaeaceae (Water lilies)

Distribution: Southern U.S.A. and Central America.
Appearance: About 16 inches (40 cm) high. Leaves sessile, decussate, elliptic, bright green, in very bright light tinged softly with red. Emergent leaves fleshy, glisten as if greasy. (Photographs page 10 and back cover, inside.)
Similar species: *Bacopa monnieri* — up to 10 inches (25 cm) tall, similar requirements; *Bacopa rotundifolia* — needs soft water, doesn't tolerate submerged culture so well as the other kinds.
Care: With light and nutrient deficiency growth is stunted, thin, lank, and pale. Regular fertilization is necessary; with CO_2-fertilization, the water can be harder, too.
Light: 50 watts per 25 gallons (100 L).
Water: 72-82°F (22-28°C); 5-15 degrees carbonate hardness; pH 6.0-7.5.
Propagation: Cuttings.
Placement: Groups in middle and background and on the sides.

Distribution: Northern South America to southern North America.
Appearance: About 20 inches (50 cm) high. Stemmed leaves, decussate, very finely pinnate with up to 600 single segments (in the aquarium often only around 200). May have floating leaves and flowers.
Care: Difficult to grow; important are: very clean water, clean ground, a great deal of light, iron fertilization. Will not tolerate hard or alkaline water. Guard against accumulated mulm and algae.
Light: 100 watts per 25 gallons (100 L).
Water: 75-82°F (24-28°C); 2-8 degrees carbonate hardness; pH 6.0-6.8.
Propagation: Cuttings.
Placement: Middle and background of high aquariums; plant in groups. Goes well with dark and large-leaved plants.
Tip: Must not be placed in an aquarium with burrowing or plant-eating fish.

Distribution: Northern South America to southern North America.
Appearance: 20 inches (50 cm) high. Leaves decussate, rarely, three-whorled ones; leaf blade finely pinnate, leaf segments about 0.04 inches (1 mm) wide, with a center vein. (Photograph on front cover.) Available in various forms commercially: Most usual are plants whose leaves are somewhat reniform in total outline, with up to 60 segments. Another form with up to 150 leaf tips and leaves that are somewhat round in total outline is often labeled *Cabomba aquatica*. The cultivated form "Silver green" is very attractive.
Care: Does not tolerate transplanting, constant pruning, and CO_2 deficiency. Needs clean water and good light.
Light: 75 watts per 25 gallons (100 L).
Water: 72-82°F (22-28°C); 2-12 degrees carbonate hardness; pH 6.5-7.2.
Propagation: Cuttings.
Placement: Background; plant in groups.

Stem Plants

Cabomba piauhyensis
Family Nymphaeaceae
(Water lilies)

Ceratophyllum demersum
Hornwort
Family Ceratophyllaceae
(Hornwort family)

Didiplis diandra (Peplis diandra)
Water purslane
Family Lythraceae
(Loosestrife family)

Distribution: Central and South America.
Appearance: About 20 inches (50 cm) high. At each stem node three leaves, leaf blade finely pinnate, rosy. In floating plants can have floating leaves and flowers. (Photograph page 30.)
Care: Soft water, strong light, and iron fertilizer are necessary. With CO_2 fertilization the water can be somewhat harder. Needs clean water and clean ground. Guard against mulm and algae. Put only gentle fish in the tank.
Light: 100 watts per 25 gallons (100 L).
Water: 75-82°F (24-28°C); 2-8 degrees carbonate hardness; pH 6.0-6.8.
Propagation: Cuttings.
Placement: In groups in middle or background. Goes well with large-leaved plants.

Distribution: World wide.
Appearance: About 20 inches (50 cm) high. Rootless plants with thick whorls of forked leaves; leaves dark-green, markedly serrated. Produces shoots freely under the water surface and branches there into a thick cushion. Can anchor itself in the ground with rootlike organs (rhizoids) from transformed leaves. (Photograph page 30.)
Care: Thin regularly; otherwise it will take light from the plants on the bottom.
Light: 35 watts or more per 25 gallons (100 L).
Water: 59-86°F (15-30°C); 5-15 degrees carbonate hardness; pH 6.0-7.5.
Propagation: Side shoots.
Placement: Anywhere in the aquarium.
Tip: Well suited to cold-water tanks and breeding tanks (good substrate for spawn and hiding places for laying females and for the young animals).

Distribution: North America.
Appearance: 6 inches (15 cm high.) Plants upright submersed, creeping emersed. Leaves decussate, bright green; tips of shoots lightly tinged with red in bright light. Small brownish flowers at the leaf axels, also in submersed culture.
Care: Branches extensively; therefore do not plant too close together. Needs good light and regular fertilization (iron).
Light: 75 watts per 25 gallons (100 L).
Water: 72-82°F (22-28°C); 2-12 degrees carbonate hardness; pH 5.8-7.2.
Propagation: Cuttings.
Placement: Close groups in foreground or in middle.

Stem Plants

Egeria (Elodea) densa
Waterweed, pondweed
Family Hydrocharitaceae
(Frog's-bit family)

Distribution: Argentina, Paraguay, Brazil.
Appearance: 20 inches (50 cm) high and higher. On free floating, somewhat brittle stems bright-green, whorled leaves, three to five to a whorl. Single leaves with very finely dentated edges. With day-light on floating shoots, whitish flowers occasionally. (Photograph page 30.)
Care: In tropical tank needs regular fertilization and much light. With CO_2 fertilization will also thrive in very hard water.
Light: 50 watts per 25 gallons (100 L).
Water: 59-77°F (15-25°C); 8-18 degrees carbonate hardness and more; pH 6.5-7.5.
Propagation: Cuttings.
Placement: Background and side portions; plant in groups.
Tip: Good oxygen producer for all aquariums. Well suited for aquariums with live-bearing killifish or American sunfish.

Heteranthera zosterifolia
Mud plaintain
Family Pontederiaceae (Pickerel weed family)

Distribution: Northern Argentina, southern Brazil, Bolivia, Paraguay.
Appearance: About 20 inches (50 cm) high. Leaves alternate, sessile, linear; thick dense leaf crown on the shoot ends. Fast-growing, extensive branching on the floating shoots, which also then sometimes bloom.
Care: Fertilize after every water change with an iron-rich fertilizer.
Light: 75 watts per 25 gallons (100 L).
Water: 72-82°F (22-28°C); 3-15 degrees carbonate hardness; pH 6.0-7.5.
Propagation: Cuttings.
Placement: On the sides and in the middle or background growing upright in loose groups; in the fore-ground as filler, for which use short cuttings (pieces of stem with a short side shoot) stuck into the ground at an angle; they produce creeping shoots in strong light.

Hydrocotyle leucocephala
Water pennywort
Family Apiaceae (Umbelliferae) (Parsley or carrot family)

Distribution: Brazil.
Appearance: About 20 inches (50 cm) high. Leaves alternate, orbicu-late to reniform with somewhat indented edges. Fine roots at the stem nodes. (Photograph page 29.)
Care: Fast-growing, groups must constantly be formed anew from end cuttings; the decapitated lower stem seldom produces new shoots and should be removed. Shoots that float on the surface branch prolifi-cally, thereby taking light from the other plants; therefore they should be regularly thinned. Needs light, otherwise undemanding.
Light: 75 watts per 25 gallons (100 L).
Water: 68-82°F (20-28°C); 2-15 degrees carbonate hardness; pH 6.0-7.5.
Propagation: Cuttings.
Placement: In groups in the back-ground or at the sides.

Stem Plants

Hygrophila corymbosa
Family Acanthaceae
(Acanthus family)

Hygrophila difformis
Water wisteria
Family Acanthaceae (Acanthus
family)

Hygrophila polysperma
Family Acanthaceae (Acanthus
family)

Distribution: India, Malaysia, Indonesia.
Appearance: About 24 inches (60 cm) high. Leaves decussate, lanceolate, like cherry leaves. Stems brown. Various forms with small, broad, and red leaf blades available commercially.
Care: Fast-growing, adaptable, but in water that is too acid the leaves are small, jaundiced, and spotted (like all _Hygrophila_ species). Regular fertilizing with iron is necessary, particularly for the red-leaved forms, which also need more light than the green. Regular cutting and new plantings. Only branches after being cut back.
Light: About 50 watts per 25 gallons (100 L).
Water: 72-82°F (22-28°C); 2-15 degrees carbonate hardness; pH 6.5-7.5.
Propagation: Cuttings.
Placement: In groups in the background or at the sides or singly — as a focus point — in small aquariums.

Distribution: India, western Indochina.
Appearance: About 20 inches (50 cm) high. Leaves decussate, stemmed. Submersed leaves deeply pinnate. Appearance varies: With cold, leaves are small, lobed instead of pinnate; with not enough light they are only slightly pinnated and internodes are long. Roots at the stem nodes. (Photographs pages 20 and 29.) Cultivated forms ("Green-white") with white veins sometimes available commercially.
Care: Needs nutrient-rich ground, regular fertilization with iron-containing fertilizer and good light; CO_2 fertilization recommended. Becomes chlorotic with iron deficiency.
Light: 75 watts per 25 gallons (100 L).
Water: 74-82°F (23-28°C); 2-15 degrees carbonate hardness; pH 6.5-7.5.
Propagation: Cuttings, runnerlike side shoots.
Placement: In groups in foreground and middle; in small aquariums also singly.

Distribution: India.
Appearance: 24 inches (60 cm) high. Leaves decussate, lanceolate, green to brownish.
Care: Branches very vigorously; therefore don't plant too close together. Prune back the groups regularly, thin, replace. Undemanding; regular fertilizing recommended.
Light: 50 watts per 25 gallons (100 L).
Water: 68-86°F (20-30°C); 2-15 degrees carbonate hardness; pH 6.5-7.8.
Propagation: Cuttings.
Placement: In groups in middle and background.

Stem Plants

Limnophila aquatica
Family Scrophulariaceae (Figwort family)

Limnophila sessiliflora
Ambulia
Family Scrophulariaceae (Figwort family)

Lobelia cardinalis
Cardinal flower
Family Lobeliaceae (Lobelia family)

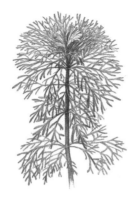

Distribution: India, Sri Lanka.
Appearance: About 20 inches (50 cm) high. Submersed leaves simple or doubly pinnate, the individual segments nearly thread thin. Leaves in three to twelve whorls, diameter of a well-developed plant up to 5 inches (12 cm).
Care: Most demanding of the *Limnophila* species, needs light, will only grow compact when light is good. Regular fertilizing with iron is necessary. Responds better to water below 8 degrees of carbonate hardness than to hard.
Light: 75 watts per 25 gallons (100 L).
Water: 75-80°F (24-27°C); 3-12 degrees carbonate hardness; pH 6.5-7.5.
Propagation: Cuttings.
Placement: Only recommended for high aquariums since the continual cutting and new planting in a shallow tank results in stunted plants. Best placed in front of a dark background. Goes well with broad-leaved, dark-green or red plants.

Distribution: Tropical Southeast Asia.
Appearance: About 20 inches (50 cm) high. Stem axis with pinnate and bifurcated leaves, which stand in 8 to 13 whorls; in good lighting the tip of the stem axis is slightly reddish. (Photograph page 29.)
Care: More adaptable to greater water hardness than is *Limnophila aquatica*. Regular iron enrichment is necessary. Very light hungry. The floating shoots on the water surface branch readily, but often are naked underneath. Renovate plantings as necessary; do not plant groups too thick.

Distribution: North America.
Appearance: About 20 inches (50 cm) high (submersed). Leaves alternate, stemmed, elliptic to obovate or spatulate, brilliant green. It occasionally produces cardinal-red blooms on long stems along the flower stalk. (Photograph page 10.)
Care: Grows slowly submersed; needs light, therefore somewhat more space needed between plants in a group; otherwise undemanding.
Light: 50 watts per 25 gallons (100 L).
Water: 68-79°F (20-26°C); 5-12 degrees carbonate hardness; pH 6.5-7.5.
Propagation: Cuttings.
Placement: In groups in middle and background as well as at the sides. Goes well with dark and red plants.
Tip: Well suited for emergent culture in large paludariums, flower windows, and in gardens. (Flower stalks to 60 inches [1.5 m] high!)
Warning: The juice that is exuded by injured plants is toxic for many kinds of fish!

Stem Plants

Ludwigia repens
False loosestrife
Family Onagraceae
(Evening primrose family)

Micranthemum micranthemoides
Family Scrophulariaceae
(Figwort family)

Myriophyllum aquaticum
Water milfoil
Family Haloragaceae
(Water milfoil family)

Distribution: Tropical North America and Central America.
Appearance: About 20 inches (50 cm) high. leaves decussate, short-stemmed, orbiculate to broad oval, upper side olive green, underside reddish to deep red; color is light-dependent — in weak light the plants remain pale. Different varieties have different growth forms. (Photograph back cover.)
Care: Prefers cool water to warm water; needs nutrient-rich ground and regular fertilization after each change of water. Branches prolifically; therefore be sure to give plants enough room when planting.
Light: 50 watts per 25 gallons (100 L).
Water: 68-86°F (20-30°C); 2-15 degrees carbonate hardness; pH 5.5-7.5.
Propagation: Cuttings.
Placement: In groups in middle and at the sides.

Distribution: Cuba, southeastern U.S.A.
Appearance: Up to 16 inches (40 cm) high. Submersed grows upright, emersed creeping. Water leaves are long ovate, sessile, whorled in threes or fours, bright green. The plants branch extensively.
Care: Plant in clusters. Needs much light, regular fertilizing. Sensitive to trypaflavin-containing fish medications and algae control products.
Light: 75 watts or more per 25 gallons (100 L).
Water: 72-82°F (22-28°C); 2-12 degrees carbonate hardness; pH 6.0-7.0.
Propagation: Cuttings.
Placement: In foreground as filler (but then cut back periodically) or in middle as small hedge. Useful for hiding the bare stems of background plants.

Distribution: South America, naturalized in southern North America.
Appearance: 20 inches (50 cm) high. Stem axis branched. Finely pinnated water leaves in three to six whorls. In good lighting the tips of the shoots are reddish. Shoots that float on the water surface can produce comblike, coarse air leaves.
Similar species: *Myriophyllum matogrossense* — with intense illumination and fertilization with iron, red-brown leaves.
Care: Don't prune too often, but thin out before they take too much light away from the ground plants. Fertilization and addition of CO_2 promote strong growth.
Light: About 50 watts per 25 gallons (100 L).
Water: 64-86°F (18-30°C); 2-15 degrees carbonate hardness; pH 5.0-7.5.
Propagation: Cuttings.
Placement: In groups in background.
Tip: Good plants for spawn.

Stem Plants

Rotala macrandra
Loosestrife
Family Lythraceae
(Loosestrife family)

Distribution: India.
Appearance: 20 inches (50 cm) high. Leaves decussate, sessile, broadly ovate to elliptic, olive-brown to dark red-brown. (Photograph back cover, inside, and back cover.)
Care: Stems and leaves sensitive to pressure. Susceptible to being eaten by snails. Strong light, fertilized ground, and regular addition of iron are necessary to maintain the red color and to deepen it. Plants grow green in weak light. Also moving water and low pH are good for the red color.
Light: 75 watts per 25 gallons (100 L).
Water: 77-86°F (25-30°C); 2-15 degrees carbonate hardness; pH 6.0-7.0.
Propagation: Cuttings.
Placement: In groups as focus point. Goes well with green plants with finely feathered leaves.
Tip: Don't use in an aquarium with lively, burrowing fish.

Rotala rotundifolia
Loosestrife
Family Lythraceae
(Loosestrife family)

Distribution: Southeast Asian mainland.
Appearance: About 20 inches (50 cm) high. Grows upright submersed, creeping emersed. Leaves decussate (rarely, in three to four whorls), form variable, mostly long oval, also small lanceolate or almost round. The tips of the shoots of these otherwise green plants can be reddish in the area of a light source. (Photograph page 10.)
Similar species: *Rotala wallichii* — leaflets needle-thin, whorled. Similar requirements but also needs soft water and pH of 5.0-6.5.
Care: Ground fertilization, regular water change and liquid iron fertilizer necessary for steady growth and reddish color.
Light: 50 watts per 25 gallons (100 L).
Water: 68-86°F (20-30°C); 2-15 degrees carbonate hardness; pH 5.5-7.2.
Propagation: cuttings.
Placement: In groups in middle and background.

Saururus cernuus
Lizard's-tail, water dragon, swamp lily
Family Saururaceae
(Lizard's-tail family)

Distribution: North America.
Appearance: Over 10 inches (25 cm) high. In aquarium, slow growing and remains small; in nature (as a marsh plant) up to 60 inches (1.5 m) tall. Leaves alternate, cordate, bright green to rich green. (Photograph back cover, inside.)
Care: Needs much light; needs fertilized ground and frequent changes of water with added nutrients. In weak light and too high a temperature poor growth. Needs regular cutting back and renewed plantings.
Light: 75 watts per 25 gallons (100 L).
Water: 64-77°F (18-25°C); 5-15 degrees carbonate hardness; pH 6.5-7.5.
Propagation: Not possible in the aquarium; in emergent culture through runners and seeds.
Placement: Foreground.
Tip: Well suited for emergent culture, grows well in garden ponds and in greenhouses.

Shinnersia rivularis
Family Asteraceae (Compositae)
(Composite family, Sunflower
family)

Eichhornia crassipes
Water hyacinth
Family Pontederiaceae
(Pickerel weed family)

Pistia stratiotes
Water lettuce, water cabbage
Family Araceae
(Arum family)

Distribution: Northern Mexico.
Appearance: 40 inches (100 cm)
high (and higher). Leaves decussate, multiple indentations at margins or deeply lobed, rich green
(cultivated forms with white veins
available commercially). Very fast
growing (up to 16 inches [40 cm]
per week), produces long internodes; in the immediate vicinity of
the light source the leaves will be
more abundant. The shoots float
and branch; new shoots over the
whole length of the stem axis.
(Photographs page 30.)
Care: Undemanding. Only recommended for large aquariums, since
otherwise weekly thinning is necessary (quickly leads to feeble
growth).
Light: 75 watts per 25 gallons
(100 L).
Water: 68-82°F (20-28°C); 2-15
degrees carbonate hardness;
pH 5.5-7.5.
Propagation: Cuttings.
Placement: In thickets or in regularly well-pruned groups in background or at the sides.

Distribution: Tropical America,
spread to tropics and subtropics all
over the world.
Appearance: About 14 inches (35
cm) high. Roots dark, very
branched. Leaves round to cordate,
leaf stems distended to globular or
oblong shape. Flowers blue,
fragrant.
Care: Floating plants for open
aquariums or for tanks with a lower
water level (large breeding aquariums). Needs about 16 inches (40
cm) of free air space over the water
surface. Does not tolerate condensation. Grows better the more the
fish fertilize the water. Requires
proper thinning (light deprivation
for ground plants).
Tip: Well suited for shade; roots
good for nest building, as spawn
substrate, and protection for new
hatchlings.
Light: At least 50 watts per 25 gallons (100 L), and best in sunlight in
the open tank.
Water: 72-79°F (22-26°C); 2-15
degrees carbonate hardness;
pH 6.0-7.8.
Propagation: Cuttings, shoots.

Distribution: Tropics and
subtropics.
Appearance: Up to 6 inches (15
cm) in diameter in sunlight, in
aquarium only up to 4 inches (10
cm) in diameter. Rosette of fleshy,
spatulate, tomentose (hairy) blue-
green leaves. In the inner leaf axil
tiny, hair white flowers. Pale to
bluish-black root ball. Grows on
the ground in shallow aquariums.
(Photographs page 30 and 40.)
Care: Will not tolerate strong heat,
no condensation. Poor growth after
being kept in the aquarium for a
long time.
Light: About 50 watts per 25 gallons (100 L).
Water: 72-79°F (2-26°C); 5-15
degrees
carbonate hardness; pH 6.5-7.5.
Propagation: Shoots.
Placement: Well suited to shade,
as spawn substrate, and for hiding.

Ferns

Bolbitis heudelotii
Family Polypodiaceae or
Lomariopsidaceae
(Polypody or Fern family)

Distribution: Ethiopia to South Africa.
Appearance: In nature up to 20 inches (50 cm) high, in the aquarium often only 8 inches (20 cm). Creeping rhizomes. Leaves stemmed, dark green, hard, somewhat brittle; leaf blade lobed and pinnate. In the wild, grows in spray zone of rushing brooks. Roots underwater, leaves emersed, entirely covered during the rainy season. (Photograph page 19).
Care: Don't plant rhizomes; better to fasten them to wood or stone (lava). For submerged maintenance, needs clean, moving water and fertilizer now and then.
Light: 30 watts per 25 gallons (100 L).
Water: 72-79°F (22-26°C); 2-12 degrees carbonate hardness; pH 5.8-7.0.
Propagation: Rhizome division or side sprouts from the rhizome.
Placement: Alone or in shady places in the background or at the side.

Ceratopteris thalictroides
Water fern, water sprite
Family Parkeriaceae
(Water fern family)

Distribution: Tropics, worldwide.
Appearance: Up to 20 inches (50 cm) tall. Dense rosette, bright green, leaves feathered and deeply cut. Large, finely branched clumps of roots. Both similar species, *Ceratopteris cornuta* and *Ceratopteris pteridoides* (floating fern) are often described as growth forms of *Ceratopteris thalictroides.* (Photograph on front cover, inside.)
Care: Fast-growing in well-fertilized water, prolific. Don't plant too deep; the beginning of the roots must be visible above the ground.
Light: 50 watts per 25 gallons (100 L).
Water: 72-86°F (22-30°C); 5-15 degrees carbonate hardness; pH 6.5-7.5.
Propagation: Adventitious plants at the left margins, very productive.
Placement: Alone or, in large aquariums, in groups in the background. Also as floating plants.

Microsorium (Polypodium)pteropus
Swordfern
Family Polypodiaceae
(Polypody or Fern family)

Distribution: Tropical Southeast Asia.
Appearance: About 8 inches (20 cm) high. Creeping rhizomes, green. Leaves single, stemmed, lanceolate, occasionally three-lobed, dark green. In the wild emergent in the spray zone of rushing streams, submersed rooted on stones or trees.(Photograph page 29.)
Care: Do not plant rhizomes; attach to stone or wood; they will grow on their own.
Light: 30 watts per 25 gallons (100 L); if necessary can do with much less.
Water: 68-82°F (20-28°C); 2-12 degrees carbonate hardness; pH 5.5-7.5.
Propagation: Adventitious plants on leaves and roots; rhizome division also possible.
Placement: Singly or in groups in foreground and middle.
Tip: Very suitable for cichlid aquariums and for dimly lighted installations.

Ferns, Liverworts, Mosses

Salvinia auriculata
Floating fern
Family Salviniaceae
(Aquatic ferns)

Distribution: Tropical America.
Appearance: Floating plant. Leaf diameter up to 0.6 inch (1.5 cm). Stems to 9 inches (20 cm) long, branching, with leaves in whorls of three. Two are developed as floating leaves, the third is a finely divided water leaf that takes over the function of the roots. (Photograph on back cover).
Care: Tolerates neither condensate nor the heat under the aquarium lid; therefore lay the cover crosswise! In deficiency of light and nutrients, grows in a stunted form that resembles the small, round-leaved *Salvinia rotundifolia*.
Light: 50 watts per 25 gallons (100 L).
Water: 68-81°F (20-27°C); 5-12 degrees carbonate hardness; pH 6.0-7.0.
Propagation: Removal of side branches.
Tip: Suitable for shadowy areas of tanks with light-sensitive fish, for small breeding tanks, and for hiding places.

Riccia fluitans
Crystalwort
Family Ricciaceae
Liverworts

Distribution: Worldwide.
Appearance: Length of a thallus (vegetative body) about 0.8 inch (2 cm). Floating plants or fastened to a substrate, flat, forked, branching thallus, which mats with others to form thick cushions. (Photograph page 19.)
Care: Undemanding; but will not long tolerate very soft, nutrient-poor water; fertilize promptly. Also avoid strong water currents made by a circulating pump.
Light: 50 watts (or less) per 25 gallons (100 L).
Water: 59-86°F (15-30°C); 5-15 degrees carbonate hardness; pH 6.0-8.0.
Propagation: Division of the mat.
Tip: Suitable for shadowed places as spawn substrate, nesting places, and protection for small juvenile fish.

Vesicularia dubyana
Java moss
Family Hypnaceae
(Mat-forming mosses)

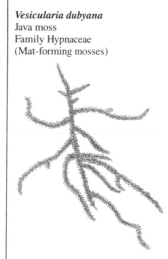

Distribution: India, Maylaya, Java.
Appearance: Single leaf up to 0.16 inch (4 mm) long. Leaf moss with thin stems and two rows of tiny lanceolate leaves. Attaches with rhizoids to stone, wood, or ground. Branches prolifically and forms thick mats.
Care: Planting not necessary; undemanding.
Light: About 25 watts per 25 gallons (100 L).
Water: 68-86°F (20-30°C); 2-15 degrees carbonate hardness; pH 5.8-7.5.
Propagation: Division of the mat.
Tip: Good for greening of wood and stones, as spawning places for bottom-spawners of all species, and for dimly lighted aquariums.

Note: In this country, most aquarium plants are referred to by their scientific names. Common names of some of the better known species are given below the scientific names, but it is *always* safer to order aquarium plants by their scientific names. These are known to the wholesalers, if not to the retailers.

Index

Index

S

Sagittaria subulata, 30, 63
Salvinia auriculata, 75
Samolus parviflorus, 19, 63
Saururus cernuus, 72
Schefflera actinophylla, 39
Self-fertile, 41
Self-sterile, 41
Sexual reproduction, 38, 41–42
Shinnersia rivularis, 30, 73
Shoots, 34
Slender-leaved Amazon, 60
Slow-release fertilizers, 33
Small aquarium, 43
Snail spawn, 24
Snails, 51
Sodium, 14
Sowing, 41–42
Spathyphyllum wallisii, 39
Spawning places, 27
Spider mites, 51
Stem axis, 6
Stem plants, 31, 65–72
Stomata, 6
Stones, 27

Storage organs, 6
Swamp lily, 72
Swamp pine, 27
Swamp plants, 7
Swordfern, 74
Swordplant, *9, 19,* 60

T

Tank size, 22
Tape grass, *29, 30*
Terraces, 27–28
Thermofilter, 17
Timer, 15
Tissue culture, 38
Trace elements, 14
　deficiency of, 53–54
Transporting plants, 23
Tubers, 6
　division of, 37

U

Underwater rose, 19, 63
Unrooted plants, 25
Unsuitable plants, 23

V

Vallisneria asiatica var. biwaensis,
　10, 64
Vallisneria gigantea, 30, 64
Vallisneria spiralis, 29, 30, 64
Vegetative reproduction, 34–38
Vesicularia dubyana, 75
Vriesia splendens, 39

W

Walls (aquarium), 27
Washington grass, 66
Water changes, 32–33
Water dragon, 72
Water fern, 74
Water hardness, 11–12
Water hyacinth, 73
Water hyssop, *10,* 66
Water lettuce, *30, 40,* 73
Water lily, *40*
Water milfoil, *39,* 71
Water pennywort, *29,* 68
Water plants. *See* Aquatic plants
Water purslane, 67
Water trumpet, 58
Water wisteria, *20, 29,* 69

Why Trust Your Pet's Health To Less Than The Best?
Depend On Our Expertise . . .
BARRON'S
PREMIUM PET CARE SERIES

- *One-volume, all-inclusive hardcover encyclopedias*
- *Written by experts in a simple, lively style*
- *Illustrated with spectacular color photographs and illustrations*

THE CAT CARE MANUAL by Bradley Viner. This comprehensive volume covers all the health needs of cats and provides insight into their instincts and behavior. Sleep patterns, hunting instincts, grooming, communication traits, and health care are detailed. 80 pages of full-color photos and 80 pages of two-color artwork. 160 pp., 7⅝" x 9¹³/₁₆," hardcover, $16.95, Can. $24.95 (5765-1)

THE DOG CARE MANUAL by David Alderton. This eminent guide book for keeping dogs healthy emphasizes proper health care and solid training by showing how to evaluate a dog's fitness and by suggesting exercises and dietary routines for canines. 80 pages of full-color photos and 80 pages of two-color artwork. 160 pp., 7⅝" x 9¹³/₁₆," hardcover, $16.95, Can. $24.95 (5764-3)

AQUARIUM FISH SURVIVAL MANUAL by Brian Ward. An easy-to-follow directory of more than 300 marine and freshwater fish species, this comprehensive book includes over 300 photos of these fabulous fish; a guide to aquatic plants, and complete instructional information about setting up and maintaining an aquarium. 176 pp., 7¾" x 10," hardcover, $18.95, NCR (5686-8)

GOLDFISH AND ORNAMENTAL CARP by Bethen Penzes and Istvan Tolg. This authoritative guide, covers everything from anatomy, biology and varieties to "housing," diet, disease and feeding. 136 pp., 7¾" x 10," hardcover, $18.95, Can. $27.95 (5634-5)

LABYRINTH FISH by Helmut Pinter. In this definitive source book, you'll learn the diets, breeding and diseases of these fish as well as aquarium maintenance. Features detailed descriptions of major aquarium species, over 60 stunning photographs, 24 drawings and 14 maps. 136 pp., 7¾" x 10," hardcover, $18.95, Can. $27.95 (5635-3)

NONVENOMOUS SNAKES by Ludwig Trutnau. This in-depth reference source features detailed descriptions of more than 100 snake species and provides the "how tos" for feeding, breeding, treating illnesses and constructing terrariums. 192 pp., 7¾" x 10," hardcover $18.95, Can. $27.95 (5632-9)

Books can be purchased at your bookstore or directly from Barron's. Enclose check or money order for total amount plus sales tax where applicable and 10% for postage. All major credit cards are accepted. Prices subject to change without notice.

Barron's Educational Series, Inc.
250 Wireless Boulevard
Hauppauge, New York 11788
For instant service call
toll-free 800-645-3476
In N.Y. call 800-257-5729
In Canada:
195 Allstate Parkway
Markham, Ontario L3R 4T8
Sales: (416) 475-9619

Perfect for Pet Owners!

PET OWNER'S MANUALS

72-80 pages, over 50 illustrations
(20-plus color photos), paperback.
AFRICAN GRAY PARROTS Wolter (3773-1)
BANTAMS Fritzsche (3687-5)
BEAGLES Vriends-Parent (3829-0)
CANARIES Frisch (2614-4)
CATS Fritzsche (2421-4)
COCKATIELS Wolter (2889-9)
DACHSHUNDS Fiedelmeier (2888-0)
DOBERMAN PINSCHERS Gudas (2999-2)
DWARF RABBITS Wegler (3669-7)
FEEDING AND SHELTERING
   EUROPEAN BIRDS von Frisch (2858-9)
FERRETS Morton (2976-3)
GERBILS Gudas (3725-1)
GERMAN SHEPHERDS Antesberger (2982-8)
GOLDEN RETRIEVERS Sucher (3793-6)
GOLDFISH Ostrow (2975-5)
GUINEA PIGS Bielfeld (2629-2)
HAMSTERS Fritzsche (2422-2)
LABRADOR RETRIEVERS Kern (3792-8)
LIZARDS IN THE TERRARIUM Jes (3925-4)
LONG-HAIRED CATS Müller (2803-1)
LOVEBIRDS Vriends (3726-X)
MICE Bielfeld (2921-9)
MYNAS von Frisch (3688-3)
NONVENOMOUS SNAKES Trutnau (5632-9)
PARAKEETS Wolter (2423-0)
PARROTS Deimer (2630-6)
PONIES Kraupa-Tuskany (2856-2)
POODLES Ullmann & Ullmann (2812-0)
RABBITS Fritzsche (2615-2)
SNAKES Griehl (2813-9)
SPANIELS Ullmann & Ullmann (2424-9)
TROPICAL FISH Braemer & Scheumann (2686-1)
TURTLES Wilkie (2631-4)
WATER PLANTS IN THE
   AQUARIUM Scheurmann (3926-2)
ZEBRA FINCHES Martin (3497-X)

NEW PET HANDBOOKS

Detailed profiles with 40 to 60 color photos.
144 pages, paperback.
NEW AQUARIUM HANDBOOK Scheurmann (3682-4)
NEW CAT HANDBOOK Müller (2922-4)
NEW DOG HANDBOOK Ullmann (2857-0)
NEW FINCH HANDBOOK Koepff (2859-7)
NEW PARAKEET HANDBOOK Birmelin & Wolter (2985-2)
NEW PARROT HANDBOOK Lantermann (3729-4)

CAT FANCIER'S SERIES

Authoritative colorful guides (over 35 color photos).
72 pages, paperback.
BURMESE CATS Swift (2925-9)
LONGHAIR CATS Pond (2923-3)
SIAMESE CATS Dunnill (2924-0)

NEW PREMIUM SERIES

Comprehensive, lavishly illustrated in color.
136-176 pages (60 to 300 color photos), hardcover.
AQUARIUM FISH SURVIVAL MANUAL Ward (5686-8)
CAT CARE MANUAL Viner (5765-1)
DOG CARE MANUAL Alderton (5764-3)
GOLDFISH AND ORNAMENTAL CARP
   Penzes & Tolg (5634-5)
LABYRINTH FISH Pinter (5635-3)

FIRST AID FOR PETS

20 pages, hardbound with hanging chain and index tabs,
fully illustrated in color.
FIRST AID FOR YOUR CAT Frye (5827-5)
FIRST AID FOR YOUR DOG Frye (5828-3)

ISBN prefix: 0-8120

Order from your favorite
book or pet store